Ethereal Explorations

Ethereal Explorations

Unraveling Ghostly Phenomena

OLIVIA K

Spectra Enterprise

CONTENTS

INDEX

INTRODUCTION

An invitation to courageous individuals to go on an enthralling voyage into the core of ghostly phenomena is extended by Ethereal Explorations, which is located at the intersection of the supernatural and that which is mysterious. This immersive experience goes beyond the bounds that are typically considered to be acceptable, and it encourages participants to discover the mysteries that lay beyond the barrier that separates the living from the afterlife.

Establishing the Occasion:

The instant as participants enter the ethereal terrain of this journey, they are immediately immersed in an atmosphere that is unearthly. An energy that cannot be seen or touched permeates the air, producing an atmosphere that has the sensation of being a tapestry that is woven with the threads of the unknown. The trip is led by seasoned experts, who are persons who are well-versed in the history, folklore, and scientific theories that surround ghosts.

One's knowledge and perceptions:

Through the course of the voyage, we will investigate the various cultural viewpoints that have influenced our concept of the afterlife. Through participation, participants are able to obtain an understanding of old legends, contemporary encounters, and the many ways in which different civilizations interpret and cope with the supernatural. It is through the sharing of a wealth of information that knowledgeable guides cultivate an awareness for the diverse array of beliefs that have been woven into the fabric of human history.

Workshops that are Interactive:

The experience of Ethereal Explorations is not one of passivity; rather, it is an opportunity to actively engage with the otherworldly. Through participation in interactive workshops, participants are immersed in the scientific procedures that are utilized in investigations of the paranormal. In order to demystify the process of detecting and speaking with spirits, participants are given the opportunity to obtain hands-on experience with several tools that are utilized by experienced investigators. These tools include electromagnetic field meters and spirit boxes.

Locations with a Haunted Past:

The ethereal environment is shown against the backdrop of ghostly locations, each of which has a distinct past that is steeped in sorrow and mystery. Dilapidated homes, ancient cemeteries, and lost ruins serve as the backdrop for adventures that are sure to send chills down your spine. Storytellers who are experts in their craft create storylines that bring the eerie history of these locations to life, transforming each step into an unforgettable adventure into the unknown.

Confronting People's Stereotypes:

With regard to the supernatural, Ethereal Explorations questions any preconceived assumptions that may exist. The participants are encouraged to approach the ethereal with both reverence and awe, which helps to cultivate an atmosphere that goes beyond fear and into a profound appreciation for the mysteries that lay beyond our grasp. It is an opportunity to rethink our perspective of the supernatural and to approach the unknown with an open mind, and the voyage provides us with this opportunity.

Reflections on the Spiritual:

Furthermore, the investigation goes beyond the realm of the physical and into the realm of the spiritual aspects of ghostly events. Participants are able to establish a connection with the energy that permeates these ethereal regions by experiencing guided meditations and engaging in spiritual reflections. Within the context of this holistic perspective, a more profound comprehension of the connectivity that exists between the living and the dead is made possible.

Methods of Conducted Investigations:

The voyage into the realm of ghostly phenomena is accompanied by an in-depth investigation into the various methods of investigation. Participants acquire the skills necessary to conduct paranormal investigations in a manner that is both thorough and ethical. An approach that is responsible and well-informed can be fostered through the acquisition of skills like the documenting of evidence, the analysis of data, and the consideration of ethical considerations when researching the mysteries of the supernatural.

Submersion in the Culture:

In addition to being an investigation, Ethereal Explorations is a cultural immersion that delves into the myriad of ways in which different communities interpret and engage with ghosts. The cultural components, rituals, and beliefs that surround death and the afterlife are investigated, which results in a more complex knowledge of the cultural fabric that shapes our interpretations of ghostly events.

Personal Developments and Changes:

More than just the expedition itself, Ethereal Explorations has an impact that transcends beyond that. Participants frequently report experiencing tremendous personal shifts, citing an increased awareness of the spiritual components of existence as the reason for their experiences. As a result of the voyage, participants are forced to confront their anxieties and preconceived notions, which ultimately results in a more meaningful connection with the mysteries of life and death. The journey serves as a catalyst for personal growth.

Considerations that are Ethical:

When conducting investigations into the paranormal, Ethereal Explorations places a significant amount of importance on ethical considerations. Participants receive direction on how to approach the supernatural while maintaining respect for the deceased and the stories they have to tell. In the course of the journey, the exploration helps to cultivate an ethical framework that strives to strike a balance between the desire of knowledge and a profound regard for the spiritual qualities that are encountered.

Inquiry Related to Science:

However, despite its profound roots in the supernatural, Ethereal Explorations also supports a scientific investigation into the occurrences that are associated with ghosts. The investigation of electromagnetic fields, variations in temperature, and other phenomena that can be measured serves as a bridge between the realms of belief and the realms of scientific understanding. The combination of scientific and spiritual viewpoints results in the development of a holistic strategy for getting to the bottom of the mysteries surrounding the ethereal.

A sense of community and connection:

The Ethereal Explorations experience is more than just a quest for an individual; rather, it is a social activity that helps players form connections with one another. Sharing experiences, engaging in collective introspection, and conducting group investigations all contribute to the formation of a sense of camaraderie that extends beyond the borders that separate the living from the dead. A one-of-a-kind and long-lasting connection is formed between the participants as a result of their joint exploration of the unknown.

Ethereal Explorations: Unraveling Ghostly Phenomena is a book that serves as a thread that connects the different aspects of human experience, from the known to the unknown. For those who have the courage to journey into the ethereal, it is an adventure that has the potential to test, enlighten, and transform them. As the participants emerge from the shadows, they take with them not only the recollections of ghostly experiences but also a profound comprehension of the connectivity that exists between the living and the dead. An invitation to uncover the secrets that go beyond the confines of the physical and to embark on a journey that goes beyond the ordinary and into the extraordinary is what Ethereal Explorations is all about.

Chapter 1

Introduction to the Unseen Realm

When we talk about the "Unseen Realm," we are referring to the dimension or realities that lie beyond the limit of our immediate perception. This realm is frequently cloaked in mystery and speculation. It embraces a wide range of ideas, ranging from the psychological and metaphysical to the spiritual and the supernatural and even further. An Unseen Realm has been investigated by a wide range of cultures, religions, and belief systems throughout the course of human history. Each of these approaches has resulted in the development of distinctive viewpoints and interpretations.

The trip into the unknown that is this examination of the Unseen Realm is an attempt to comprehend the unseen forces that have the potential to influence our world and existence. It entails the investigation of worlds that exist beyond the physical, realms that exist in the voids between what we can see, touch, and comprehend. The purpose of this introduction is to present a full overview of the Unseen Realm, including a discussion of its significance in terms of culture, religion, and philosophy, as well as its contemporary relevance in relation to the breakthroughs in science and technology.

Perspectives from the Past on the Realm That Cannot Be Seen
Traditions and Mythology of Ancient Civilizations
There is a strong connection between the concept of an Unseen Realm and the mythology and cosmologies of ancient civilizations across the world. A number of Mesopotamian societies held the belief that the gods inhabited a heavenly world and exercised their authority over the affairs of human beings. In a similar manner, ancient Egyptian beliefs featured the concept of an afterlife as well as the existence of spiritual forces that influenced the fates of individuals.

The Greeks, with their pantheon of gods that resided on Mount Olympus, and the Romans, with their concept of numina occupying sacred sites, both added to the rich tapestry of the Unseen Realm. Both of these civilizations brought their own unique perspectives to the table. There was a gap between what could be seen and what could not be seen, and these ancient civilizations bridge that gap by using myths and stories to explain the invisible forces that were at work in the world.

Perspectives from the Religious

All of the major faiths of the world provide profound understandings of the Unseen Realm. The Bible, which is the central text of Christianity, contains descriptions of angels, demons, and a spiritual realm that is intertwined with the material world. The Christian conception of the Unseen Realm is made more complicated by the presence of the concepts of heaven and hell, as well as the concept of a divine design.

There is a discussion in the Quran about jinn, which are beings that are produced from smokeless fire, and these beings' interactions with mankind. In addition, the Islamic worldview incorporates the belief in angels and the existence of an afterlife, which further broadens the scope of the Unseen.

Karma, reincarnation, and a variety of heavenly realms that are inhabited by deities and other supernatural entities are some of the themes that are introduced in the elaborate cosmologies of Hinduism and Buddhism. Throughout various traditions, the complicated web of gods, goddesses, and other spiritual entities adds to the creation of an Unseen Realm that is both rich and diverse.

In addition to the Mystical and Metaphysical Dimensions
Metaphysics and philosophical thought

There are a variety of intellectual and metaphysical perspectives that, in addition to religious traditions, investigate the Unseen Realm. Plato's Allegory of the Cave investigates the concept that the reality that we perceive is nothing more than shadows on the wall, indicating that there is a higher, more significant truth. In a similar vein, traditional Eastern philosophies like Taoism and Zen Buddhism place a strong emphasis on the significance of transcending the visible world in order to get a more profound comprehension of reality.

The idea of the Unseen Realm is frequently brought up in metaphysical discourse, and it frequently incorporates conversations about awareness, the nature of life, and the interconnection of everything. Philosophical frameworks were supplied by visionaries such as Immanuel Kant and Friedrich Nietzsche. These frameworks questioned the boundaries of human perception and explored realms that went beyond the physical.

The Traditions of Mysticism

For a very long time, mystic traditions from all different civilizations have been trying to break through the curtain that separates the visible and the invisible. The cultivation of a connection with higher realms of awareness is the goal of practices such as meditation, prayer, and rituals. Experiences of encountering spirits or divine energies that exist beyond the corporeal world are frequently reported by mystics and others who are seeking spiritual enlightenment.

Kabbalah is a branch of Judaism that is considered to be mystical. It investigates the nature of God, the cosmos, and the interconnectedness of everything in the universe.

In a similar vein, Sufism, which is a branch of Islam, places an emphasis on having a direct personal experience of the divine, which transcends the boundaries of the secular world.

The Importance of Contemporary Issues and Scientific Investigations
Phenomena and Anomalies of a Paranormal Nature

It is via reports of supernatural occurrences that the Unseen Realm continues to captivate the imagination of those living in the modern world. Ghost sightings, near-death experiences, and encounters with unidentified flying objects (UFOs) are all occurrences that generate issues regarding the nature of reality and the existence of dimensions that are not visible to the naked eye.

Within the realm of science, investigations into supernatural occurrences frequently involve the investigation of topics such as quantum physics, consciousness, and the nature of time. The concept of parallel universes, multiverse ideas, and the possibility of realms that are beyond our current comprehension are all topics that are discussed by researchers and scientists.

The Mind-Body Connection and the Concept of Consciousness

There is a relationship between the investigation of the Unseen Realm and the study of consciousness as well as the connection between the mind and the body. The notion of consciousness as a reality that goes beyond the physical body challenges conventional materialistic beliefs. This understanding may be traced back to ancient contemplative practices and continues to be at the forefront of modern neuroscientific research.

New disciplines of study, such as neurotheology, are investigating the cerebral foundation of spiritual experiences. These studies indicate the possibility that the Unseen Realm may have correlations within the human brain through their findings. At the point where science and spirituality meet, there are opportunities for discourse and investigation into the nature of reality and the possibility of the presence of dimensions that are not visible to the naked eye.

Representations of Culture and Popular Culture of the World
Art, Literature, and Motion Pictures

There are many different ways in which the Unseen Realm might be expressed through human creativity. Frequently, themes that are associated with the supernatural, the mystical, and the unseen are investigated in works of literature, art, and film. As a canvas for human imagination, the Unseen Realm is used in a wide variety of works of literature, ranging from long-standing works such as Dante's "Divine Comedy" to contemporary works of fantasy literature and film.

In particular, the genre of fantasy gives authors the opportunity to construct entire worlds with their own rules, magic systems, and forces that cannot be seen. J.R.R. Tolkien's Middle-earth and J.K. Rowling's Wizarding World are two examples of works that bring to life places that are beyond the ordinary. These works invite readers to examine the presence of the Unseen in their own lives.

Legends and folklore from the streets

There is a cultural lens that is provided by folklore and urban legends, which allows for the perception of the Unseen Realm. People all throughout the world have a collective imagination that is filled with stories about supernatural entities, legendary creatures, and haunted places. The purpose of these tales is frequently to act as cautionary tales, reflections on societal worries, or attempts to make sense of everything that is unknown.

There are urban stories that contribute to the contemporary folklore that surrounds the Unseen Realm. These urban legends can be about cryptids like Bigfoot or encounters with alien creatures. The ubiquity of such legends is a reflection of humanity's everlasting interest with the unexplained and the inexplicable.

Despite the fact that it is as old as human civilization itself, the concept of the Unseen Realm continues to captivate and inspire people. Whether it be through religious beliefs, philosophical inquiries, scientific explorations, or cultural representations, the concept of dimensions that exist beyond our immediate perspective continues to be an essential component of the human experience.

The purpose of this introduction is to provide a brief overview of a broad and complex subject matter, which encourages further investigation and reflection. As we make our way through the complexity of the seen and the unseen, we set out on a voyage that goes beyond the borders of culture, religion, and science; it is a journey that aims to uncover the mysteries of the Unseen Realm.

1.1 Setting the Stage: The fascination with the paranormal

The fascination with the supernatural has been a part of human civilization for a very long time, and it has persisted regardless of the passage of time, geographical location, or belief system. Over the course of human history, people have been fascinated by the supernatural, the unexplained, and the strange. This fascination has persisted from ancient civilizations to the modern world. The purpose of this investigation is to investigate the elements that contribute to the ongoing fascination that people have with the supernatural. These considerations include cultural, psychological, and societal aspects that play a role in the observation of this fascinating phenomena.

Fascination with the Paranormal and Its Cultural Origins
Mythology and the Beliefs of Former Times

It is possible to trace the origins of our curiosity with the supernatural back to the mythology and belief systems that were prevalent in ancient civilizations. In societies where natural occurrences were frequently attributed to the actions of gods, spirits, or other supernatural entities, the paranormal was an essential component of the worldview that was prevalent in those societies. With their storylines that frequently contained interactions with gods, monsters, and otherworldly forces, myths served as a means of providing an explanation for things that could not be explained without them.

By way of illustration, in Greek mythology, tales of mythical animals such as the Sphinx and the Minotaur, as well as stories of gods descending from Mount Olympus to engage with people, expressed a preoccupation with the line between the visible and the invisible. In a similar vein, ancient Egyptian beliefs in the afterlife and the reality of spirits mingling with the living highlighted a profound sense of interaction with the supernatural.

Folklore and the Traditions of Many Cultures

Through folklore and cultural traditions, the long-standing curiosity with the supernatural has endured throughout the development of societies. There are numerous instances of ghosts, spirits, and other supernatural beings that may be found in folk tales from all across the world. In many cases, these tales, which were handed down from generation to generation, served various goals, including providing entertainment, imparting moral lessons, and providing explanations for natural events that were beyond the comprehension of the period.

Additionally, elements of the supernatural were regularly interwoven into both cultural customs and rituals, as well as festivities.

In a cultural context where the paranormal was not only feared but rather welcomed as an inherent part of the human experience, festivals that were dedicated to the dead, rituals that were used to communicate with spirits, and rites that were held to fend off malicious forces all contributed to the same cultural landscape.

Fascination with the Paranormal and Its Psychological Considerations
Fear, as well as the Unknown

There is a strong connection between fear and the unknown, which is one of the underlying psychological characteristics that drives people's attraction with the paranormal. At the same time that the human psyche is hardwired to be cautious and vigilant in the face of uncertainty, the paranormal symbolizes a realm that defies rational explanation. When combined, the fear of the unknown and the excitement of adventure produce a potent concoction that has the ability to captivate the mind of a human being.

This dread is not always a negative emotion; in fact, it frequently functions as a defense mechanism for survival. When applied to the realm of the supernatural, it can take the form of awe and astonishment, which drives people to search for comprehension and significance in the face of phenomena that cannot be explained using ordinary methods.

An insatiable curiosity and a search for meaning

The paranormal presents an unending frontier for exploration, which is a natural trait of human beings because of their intrinsic curiosity. In the pursuit of understanding the mysteries of the unseen, individuals have been compelled to explore the boundaries of knowledge through a variety of means, including scientific research, personal experiences, and narrative.

A never-ending search for meaning is encouraged by the paranormal, which includes mysterious occurrences like ghosts, unidentified flying objects (UFOs), and psychic skills. The paranormal becomes a domain where the mystical and the scientific collide, creating a potential bridge between the known and the unknowable. People are looking for solutions to existential issues, and the paranormal becomes a realm where this intersection occurs.

Aspects of Society and Technology That Have an Impact
Media and the Culture of the People

There is no possible way to overestimate the significance of the media and popular culture in the process of generating and maintaining interest with the supernatural.

A big part in the dissemination of paranormal narratives to an audience all over the world has been played by many mediums, including books, films, television shows, and now digital platforms. Iconic works such as "Frankenstein" by Mary Shelley and "Dracula" by Bram Stoker lay the groundwork for a literary obsession with the supernatural that continues to develop to this day.

The introduction of radio and television in the 20th century introduced supernatural tales into people's homes for the first time because of its accessibility. "The Twilight Zone" and "The X-Files" were two examples of television programs that grabbed audiences with their stories of the strange and inexplicable. In today's world, the democratization of paranormal storytelling is facilitated by online platforms, podcasts, and social media. These developments make it possible for individuals to communicate their own personal experiences and theories.

Recent Developments in Technology and the Investigation of the Paranormal

A further factor that has contributed to the rise in interest in the supernatural is the progression of technology. Electromagnetic field (EMF) meters, infrared cameras, and voice recorders are examples of tools that have proven indispensable in the realm of paranormal investigations. The convergence of scientific inquiry with the supernatural, as represented by television programs such as "Ghost Hunters," has resulted in the emergence of a subculture consisting of novice and experienced paranormal investigators.

The widespread availability of cellphones has made it simpler for folks to record and discuss events that they believe to be related to the paranormal. A communal consciousness that is becoming more receptive to the notion of the supernatural is being contributed to by the widespread dissemination of photographs, films, and audio recordings on social media platforms.

Phenomena of the Paranormal in the Present Day
Unidentified Flying Objects and Extraterrestrial Life

In recent years, the fascination with the paranormal has found expression in the increasing interest in UFOs (Unidentified Flying Objects) and the search for extraterrestrial life. Both of these topics have captured the attention of thousands of people. Disclosures made by the government, papers that have been declassified, and the testimonials of military personnel have all contributed to the public's level of interest and conjecture over the presence of mysterious aerial phenomena.

The combination of science, government secrets, and the unknown has captivated the imagination of the general people, which has led to conversations about the potential repercussions that could result from making contact with alien intelligence. Our curiosity with the unknown is heightened by a confluence of sociological, technological, and psychological elements, which are all contributing to the contemporary phenomena of unidentified flying objects (UFOs).

Hauntings and Paranormal Investigations

There has been a rise in the popularity of ghost hunting, which involves people and organizations going to places that are said to be haunted in the hopes of finding evidence of supernatural activity. Television shows and other platforms that feature investigations in supposedly haunted locations contribute to the normalizing of paranormal inquiry by showcasing the findings of these investigations.

The practice of ghost hunting has become more accessible to the general public as a result of the growth of EVP (Electronic Voice Phenomena) equipment and thermal imaging cameras. This has made it possible for enthusiasts to conduct their own investigations into the paranormal. There is a participatory aspect to the fascination with ghosts and hauntings, which means that the appeal of connecting with the supernatural and capturing evidence of an unseen realm adds a layer of participation.

When it comes to navigating the uncharted territory

The obsession with the supernatural is a multidimensional phenomenon that has profound roots in the history of humanity as well as in some aspects of psychology. Ancient mythology and modern sightings of unidentified flying objects (UFOs) are just two examples of how the paranormal continues to be a source of fascination, horror, and wonder. We are compelled to explore the undiscovered frontiers of the human experience as a result of the intersection of cultural, psychological, and sociological variables, which are all aspects that intensify our curiosity about the unknown.

As we make our way through this obsession, it is of the utmost importance that we acknowledge the various ways in which the paranormal shows itself in different cultures and individuals. The research of the paranormal continues to be a dynamic and ever-evolving component of the human journey, regardless of whether it is motivated by a search for meaning, a curiosity with the unknown, or a need to confront our anxieties. We find a space where creativity, curiosity, and the unknown merge when we are confronted with the inexplicable; this is a space that continues to capture and inspire the human spirit.

1.2 Historical Perspectives: Ghosts in culture and folklore

Since the beginning of time, ghosts, which are ethereal entities that are thought to be the spirits of the deceased, have been a significant part of the folklore, mythologies, and cultural beliefs of various civilizations throughout the course of human history. Over the course of history, the concept of ghosts has evolved into a wide variety of manifestations and interpretations, transcending both geographical and cultural boundaries. In this investigation, historical viewpoints on ghosts are investigated, and the roles that ghosts play in cultural narratives, religious beliefs, and the human psyche are investigated throughout.

Ghosts in the Cultures of the Past

Ancient Egypt and Mesopotamia

The cultures of Mesopotamia and Egypt, which are considered to be the cradle of civilization, were the ones that lay the foundation for beliefs in the afterlife and spirits. The Mesopotamians held the belief that there were spirits that roamed the earth and could cause chaos if they were not appeased by ceremonies with their presence. Ghosts were seen by the Egyptians as souls that were looking for resolution or passage to the other side of the afterlife. This was due to the Egyptians' complex beliefs regarding the afterlife. Extensive burial rituals and tomb inscriptions were performed with the intention of ensuring that the souls of the deceased had a peaceful passage.

Tradition of the Greco-Romans

In ancient Greece and Rome, the concept of ghosts went through a number of different stages of development. After death, it was believed that the shadows of the deceased lingered in the Underworld, and rites such as necromancy were performed in an attempt to connect with these spirits. The contacts with the supernatural were portrayed as both cautionary tales and reflections of the human condition in Greek plays and Roman literature. Ghost stories found expression in both of these literary genres.

Religious traditions that involve ghosts

Religion of Hinduism

The concept of ghosts is included into the cosmology of Hinduism, which is characterized by a profoundly diverse collection of tales and beliefs. When souls who have passed away are unable to find peace, they may transform into ghosts and wander the realm of the living. Various rituals, like the Shraddha ceremony, are performed with the intention of bringing these souls comfort and making their journey to the hereafter easier. In the context of the notion of bhoota preta, which refers to restless spirits, the need of soothing the deceased is emphasized.

Buddhism

Because Buddhism places such a strong emphasis on reincarnation and karma, it recognizes the presence of ghosts or hungry spirits, which are referred to as preta. Unfulfilled wishes or negative karma are considered to be the driving forces behind these spirits, which are believed to reside in a realm of pain. The purpose of Buddhist practices, which include the creation of merit and the performance of ceremonies, is to ease the suffering of these spirits and to direct them toward a more favorable rebirth.

A Christian faith

Within the framework of Christian beliefs, the concept of ghosts is intricately connected with ideas of the afterlife, sin, and salvation. It is possible to view ghosts as souls imprisoned in purgatory, where they are purified before being allowed to enter heaven. Adding a supernatural element to Christian theology is the notion that saints or the Virgin Mary might appear to believers in the form of apparitions. It is common for ghost stories to have both moral and religious goals, with the primary focus being on the implications that one's actions will have in the hereafter.

It is Islam

Jinn, which are supernatural entities produced from smokeless fire, are included in the concept of spirits that are incorporated into Islamic beliefs alongside other supernatural beings. There is a possibility that jinn or deceased individuals are connected to ghost-like entities that are referred to as arwah. In order to address problems that are believed to be caused by harmful spirits, Islamic exorcism rituals known as Ruqyah are performed. These rituals call attention to the significance of seeking protection through prayer and the recital of the Quran.

Ghosts Within the Cultures of Asia

Japanese and Chinese customs and practices

A large number of ghost stories can be found in Chinese folklore. These ghost stories are frequently associated with themes of unfinished business or unresolved emotions. There is a famous Chinese tradition known as the Hungry Ghost Festival, which involves the making of offerings in order to satisfy wandering ghosts. Within the realm of Japanese tradition, yūrei are resentful ghosts that seek justice or retribution. There are many stories of supernatural horror that represent these ghosts, which are depicted with particular characteristics such as long disheveled hair and a white burial gown. These ghosts frequently harass the living.

Some Beliefs of Southeast Asians

The cultural viewpoints on ghosts that are prevalent throughout Southeast Asia have been influenced by animistic beliefs.

It is normal practice to acknowledge the existence of nature spirits or the spirits of ancestors, and ceremonies are regularly carried out in order to honor and pacify these entities. Ghost stories in these cultures frequently depict a profound connection between the natural and spiritual realms, highlighting the significance of preserving harmony with the forces that cannot be seen.

According to European folklore, ghosts

Traditions from the Highlands and Norse

From the perspective of Celtic legend, ghosts were thought to be the spirits of the deceased who were able to return to the realm of the living. There was a period when people felt that the line between the living and the dead was not as clear as it is today, and Samhain was the precursor of Halloween as we know it today. A number of spectral entities were also present in Norse mythology. These included the draugr, which were undead beings who had a strong desire for vengeance. These traditions had an impact on the way people in medieval Europe viewed ghosts and other supernatural phenomena.

Medieval and Renaissance Europe in Europe

During the Middle Ages in Europe, Christian beliefs and folk traditions began to entwine with one another, which resulted in the creation of tales around supernatural happenings and restless spirits. The fear of unquiet souls returning to the living world and the concept of purgatory were primary influences on the development of medieval ghost mythology. In the course of the Renaissance, there was a growing fascination with esoteric knowledge and the occult, which led to the investigation of mystical aspects and further influenced the way people in different cultures viewed ghosts.

The Development of Ghost Stories throughout Time

Literature that is Gothic

Gothic literature, which embraced themes of the macabre and the otherworldly, is said to have flourished during the 18th and 19th centuries. Authors such as Edgar Allan Poe and Mary Shelley conducted research into the more sinister aspects of the human experience, frequently incorporating spectral figures or ghosts into their works. Some of the factors that contributed to the rise in popularity of ghost stories as a literary genre were the spooky atmospheres and haunting settings that were popularized by Gothic tales.

Spiritism in the Victorian Era

During the Victorian era, there was a rise of interest in spiritualism, which is a movement that focuses on connecting with the deceased. There was a growing interest in the afterlife and the prospect of making touch with the spirit world, which led to the rise in popularity of séances, mediums, and ghost photography. During the time that spiritualism was gaining believers as well as skeptics, the line that separated science and the supernatural became increasingly hazy.

Specters in Contemporary Culture

Ghost Stories from the Modern Era

With the introduction of film, television, and literature in the 20th and 21st centuries, the depiction of ghosts in popular culture has gradually developed over the course of these two centuries. Contemporary narratives frequently investigate psychological and existential themes, despite the fact that traditional ghost stories continue to remain popular. Reflecting the shifting viewpoints of the modern period, ghosts may represent unresolved pain, guilt, or society worries. Ghosts may also represent societal anxieties.

Investigations into the Paranormal

The obsession with ghosts has expanded beyond the realm of storytelling and into the realm of active exploration through the investigation of paranormal phenomena. Individuals and organizations that are armed with technology such as electromagnetic field (EMF) meters, infrared cameras, and voice recorders are attempting to gather evidence of paranormal activity. Television series and documentaries that feature actual ghost hunting have gained broad appeal, which has contributed to the normalization of the examination of paranormal phenomena.

In their capacity as cultural archetypes, ghosts continue to hold a stronghold on the human mind. Throughout history, ghosts have been used as symbolic representations of the human experience. These representations range from ancient beliefs that are based on the mysteries of the afterlife to contemporary depictions that are influenced by psychological and existential issues. Not only does the development of ghost stories reflect shifts in cultural attitudes, but it also represents the everlasting fascination with the unknown, the strange, and the mysteries that lie beyond the veil of mortality. We are able to untangle the connections that bind us to the ageless narratives of the ethereal and the unseen when we investigate historical perspectives on ghosts.

1.3 The Intersection of Science and the Supernatural

Throughout the course of human history, the relationship between science and the supernatural has been a topic of intrigue, discussion, and investigation. The domain of the supernatural encompasses events that go beyond the limitations of what can be observed and what can be measured, in contrast to the scientific endeavor, which strives to gain an understanding of the natural world via the use of reason and empirical scientific observation. Through the examination of historical viewpoints, contemporary conversations, and the ongoing attempt to reconcile empirical inquiry with the mysteries that lay beyond the realm of the ordinary, this investigation explores beyond the surface of the intricate junction of science and the supernatural.

The Evolution of Alchemy and Natural Philosophy from a Historical Perspective

The occult and the practice of alchemy

The practice of alchemy is a perfect example of how the borders between science and the supernatural were flexible throughout the pre-modern era due to the fact that the limits were fluid. The goal of alchemists was not only to transform base metals into gold, but also to discover the secrets of immortality and to communicate with spiritual entities. The border between the empirical and the metaphysical was frequently blurred by the esoteric language and symbols that alchemists utilized in their work.

In a similar manner, the investigation of the occult was linked with the pursuit of early scientific knowledge. In addition to engaging in scientific investigation, individuals such as John Dee, who was a mathematician, astronomer, and counselor to Queen Elizabeth I, also participated in occult rituals such as scrying and angelic communication. It is a reflection of a worldview in which the borders between the natural and the supernatural were porous and the historical roots of science were intertwined with mystical and esoteric traditions.

Philosophy of Nature and the Beginning of the Scientific Revolution

One of the most significant turning points in the connection between science and the supernatural occurred during the Scientific Revolution, which coincided with the birth of modern science. Even though they made significant contributions to the fields of physics and mathematics, visionaries like Isaac Newton continued to have an interest in subjects such as alchemy and biblical prophecy. It was a more comprehensive view of the natural world that incorporated both scientific research and metaphysical speculation, and the phrase "natural philosophy" covered this comprehensive understanding.

The more methodical procedures of contemporary science, which place an emphasis on empirical observation, experimentation, and the formation of hypotheses that can be tested, progressively replaced alchemy as the dominant scientific approach. The Scientific Revolution set the groundwork for a scientific worldview that sought to explain natural occurrences through rational inquiry. This paradigm eventually led to the progressive separation of science from components that were blatantly supernatural.

A Skeptical Perspective on the Enlightenment
Rationalism of the Enlightenment

During the Enlightenment, the separation between science and the supernatural became even more firmly established. Reason, skepticism, and empirical evidence were the three pillars of scientific inquiry that were championed by various thinkers during the Enlightenment. A more secular and rationalistic approach to comprehending the natural world was made possible as a result of the rejection of superstition and dogma.

René Descartes and Immanuel Kant were two of the prominent figures who contributed to the development of a mechanical view of the cosmos. This perspective held that natural laws were responsible for governing the behavior of matter. The supernatural was assigned to the realm of personal belief, which was kept distinct from the empirical research that occurred inside the scientific community.

Uncertainty in the Scientific Community

The level of skepticism that was directed toward claims of supernatural phenomena increased as scientific procedures got more rigorous. Within the context of the development of scientific skepticism, the critical study of paranormal phenomena, miracles, and claims of supernatural occurrences was a crucial component. The credibility of eyewitness testimony was called into question by academics such as David Hume, who also emphasized the significance of empirical evidence when judging statements that were considered to be remarkable.

Skepticism in the scientific community, while necessary for preserving the credibility of the scientific method, also resulted in the inflexible rejection of phenomena that did not conform to the paradigm that had been created. At the junction of science and the supernatural, discussions continue to be shaped by the tension that exists between the rigor of scientific inquiry and the open-mindedness of inquiry.

Psychic Phenomena and Parapsychology Through the Lens of Contemporary Dialogues
One of the Scientific Disciplines That Is Parapsychology

As a result of the investigation of psychic occurrences that took place during the 19th and 20th centuries, the field of parapsychology came into being. The study of extrasensory perception (ESP), telekinesis, and other occurrences that appeared to defy standard scientific explanations was the focus of parapsychologists, who attempted to apply scientific procedures to the investigation of these events.

In the latter half of the 19th century, there was a growing interest in studying claims of the paranormal using scientific principles, which led to the founding of organizations such as the Society for Psychical Research (SPR). Parapsychology, on the other hand, encountered obstacles in its pursuit of universal recognition within the scientific community. These obstacles included methodological difficulties, problems with replication, and the extremely contentious nature of the phenomenon that was being investigated.

Why Psi Phenomena Presents Such a Challenge

Psychic phenomena, which include telepathy, clairvoyance, and precognition, pose a unique challenge to the conventional scientific paradigms that have been practiced for centuries. However, the reproducibility of such findings continues to be a difficult subject, despite the fact that certain research has suggested that there are statistically significant results that support the presence of psi. The lack of a theoretical framework that is in line with the principles that have been established in the scientific community continues to be a source of skepticism, with critics pointing to methodological errors.

Examples of the constant conflict that exists at the junction of science and the supernatural can be seen in the conversation that takes place between skeptics and parapsychologists. Skeptics maintain a commitment to methodological rigor and seek substantial evidence before contemplating the inclusion of paranormal events within the scientific framework. This is in contrast to the position taken by parapsychologists, who argue for the significance of open-minded research and the exploration of unexplored territory.

Consciousness and Quantum Physics respectively
A Look at Reality and Quantum Mechanics

The introduction of quantum physics in the early 20th century ushered in a period of profound change in our comprehension of the underlying nature of reality.

Wave-particle duality, non-locality, and the observer effect are some of the characteristics that define quantum events. These phenomena posed a challenge to the traditional concepts of determinism and objectivity.

As a result of the implications of quantum physics, philosophical arguments were held about the nature of consciousness and the role that it plays in the formation of reality. It was specifically the observer effect that suggested that the act of observation could have an effect on the behavior of subatomic particles. These quantum puzzles have been seized upon by certain individuals who advocate for the junction of science and the supernatural in order to establish linkages between consciousness and the manipulation of reality.

What Is the Problem with Consciousness?

One of the most important and unsolved puzzles in the field of science is the interaction that exists between consciousness and the material universe. The scientific community continues to exercise caution when it comes to deriving metaphysical conclusions from the intricacies of quantum events, despite the fact that quantum physics has spurred speculative conversations regarding the role of consciousness in shaping reality.

The discussion that surrounds quantum physics and consciousness exemplifies the difficulties that arise when attempting to navigate the borders between scientific investigation and metaphysical interpretation. The pursuit of understanding the nature of consciousness and the possible connections it may have with the domain of the supernatural continues to be the driving force behind interdisciplinary questions that are at the forefront of scientific and philosophical discourse.

Technology in Relation to the Otherworldly
Investigating the Paranormal in the Age of Digital Technology

Current conversations at the convergence of science and the supernatural have been significantly influenced by technological advancements, which have played a vital part in molding these conversations. The proliferation of instruments like electromagnetic field (EMF) meters, infrared cameras, and digital voice recorders has made it easier for people to engage in the practice of paranormal inquiry, which has become increasingly popular.

Bringing the methods and tools of scientific research into the public domain has been accomplished through the use of television shows and online platforms that are dedicated to the investigation of paranormal phenomena. Nevertheless, the scientific rigor of many amateur investigations has been called into doubt.

This is due to the fact that the subjective interpretation of evidence and the absence of controlled settings frequently hamper the trustworthiness of conclusions generated by these investigations.

An Artificial Intelligence System and the Detection of Anomalies

A unique convergence of technology and the supernatural is represented by the incorporation of artificial intelligence (AI) into the examination of paranormal phenomena. When it comes to analyzing massive datasets of audio, video, and environmental sensor data, artificial intelligence algorithms are being utilized to search for abnormalities that may suggest the presence of paranormal activity. While the application of artificial intelligence does bring about a degree of impartiality, the issue lies in the development of algorithms that are able to accurately differentiate between true abnormalities and natural changes in the environment.

Confronting the Obstacles of Reconciliation
An Oversight of the Gulf

A fundamental difficulty is presented by the junction of science and the supernatural, which is the question of how to reconcile the empirical rigor of scientific investigation with the intrinsically mysterious and unobservable nature of the domain of the supernatural. A nuanced approach that takes into account the limitations of human perception, the ever-changing nature of scientific paradigms, and the possibility of events that defy existing understanding is required in order to bridge this gap.

Inquiry with an Open Mind

It is necessary for the scientific community to maintain an open-minded inquiry in order to stimulate innovation and investigate phenomena that may question the paradigms that are already in place. It is essential to be willing to accept new ideas without an excessive amount of skepticism in order to push the boundaries of knowledge. Throughout the course of academic history, scientific fields have been subject to paradigm shifts.

Extremely Strict Methodology

On the other hand, advocates of the scientific method support the use of rigorous methodology and emphasize the significance of skepticism as a means of protecting against pseudoscience and assertions that are not supported by evidence. The creation of testable hypotheses, systematic observation, and the replication of results are all components of the scientific process, which is a framework aimed to reduce the likelihood of errors and biases when conducting research.

Matters with Ethical Implications

Additionally, ethical questions are brought up by the convergence of scientific research with the supernatural. The necessity for ethical principles within the scientific community as well as the community of people who investigate the paranormal is brought to light by the possibility of exploiting vulnerable persons through pseudoscientific methods, the falsification of evidence, and the manipulation of belief systems.

A conversation that is continuous and ever-evolving continues to take place at the confluence of science and the supernatural. From the historical entanglements of alchemy and natural philosophy to the present investigations of quantum consciousness and AI-assisted paranormal research, the desire to understand the inexplicable and unexplained continues to be a persistent endeavor.

In order to successfully navigate this intersection, it is necessary to strike a delicate balance between scientific rigor and open-minded curiosity. New frontiers are emerging as our understanding of the natural world continues to develop. These new frontiers present us with the challenge of exploring the unknown with humility, skepticism, and a true commitment to unraveling the mysteries that lie at the confluence of science and the supernatural. The continuing conversation extends an invitation to all individuals, including scientists, philosophers, and enthusiasts, to participate in a collective adventure of discovery. This trip will continue to investigate and redefine the boundaries between what can be observed and other things that cannot be observed.

Chapter 2

Ghostly Manifestations and Haunting Patterns

The universe of ghostly manifestations and haunting patterns is like a tapestry of mystery, dread, and intrigue that is sewn together with threads of these emotions. The legends of ghosts, apparitions, and haunted locations have been passed down from generation to generation, resulting in a complex tapestry of paranormal events. These tales have been passed down across cultures and countries throughout history. In the course of this investigation, we dig into the multifaceted world of ghostly manifestations, analyzing common patterns, cultural variances, and making an effort to solve the mystery of the supernatural.

What Makes Ghostly Manifestations Are What They Are
Illusions and Spirits of the Past

When ghosts present themselves, they frequently take the form of apparitions, which are ethereal entities that appear to live people. It is typical for people to describe seeing these apparitions in places that have a significant historical value, have experienced tragic occurrences, or have strong emotional imprints. These apparitions can range from transparent figures to completely embodied creatures.

There are many different cultural situations in which people think that spirits are the essence of those who have departed dead. It is possible for these beings to remain in the domain of the living due to emotions that have not been resolved, unfinished business, or a wish to contact those who are still alive. There are a variety of sensory experiences that can accompany the apparition of spirits. These experiences might include visual sightings, audio events, and even tactile communication with the spirits.

Phenomena and Poltergeists in the Physical World

Poltergeists are creatures that are related to physical disturbances. The term "poltergeist" originates from the German terms "poltern" (which means "to make noise") and "geist" (which means "spirit"). In contrast to traditional ghosts, poltergeists are characterized by their capacity to exert influence over the surrounding physical environment. In addition to the manifestation of physical pain, such as wounds or bruises, common manifestations include sounds that cannot be explained, items that move or levitate, and even the manifestation of sound.

There has been much discussion within the field of paranormal research over the characteristics of poltergeist activity. Some people believe that these phenomena are the result of external spiritual entities, while others believe that they are the consequence of humans' unconscious psychokinetic talents.

Certain Recurring Themes and Patterns of Haunting

There are still hauntings

The recurrence of particular occurrences or feelings that are connected to a particular area is a defining characteristic of residual hauntings. It's almost as if a moment in time has been imprinted on the surroundings, and when specific conditions are met, this imprint can be heard as if it were a spectral recording. It is possible for witnesses to residual hauntings to see apparitions or experience sensory experiences that are related with the events that left the psychic imprint.

Hauntings are frequently associated with traumatic or emotionally charged events, such as battles, murders, or powerful emotional experiences. These hauntings are typically tied to. It appears that the beings that are involved in residual hauntings do not interact with one another; rather, they appear to exist as imprints on the fabric of existence and time.

Hauntings that are Intelligent

Whereas residual hauntings involve creatures that appear to possess self-awareness and the ability to engage with the living, intelligent hauntings involve entities that appear to have the ability to interact with the living. It is possible for these creatures to react to stimuli from the outside world, communicate with one another through a variety of channels (such as EVP, which stands for electronic voice phenomena), and even exhibit a degree of consciousness.

It is common practice to attribute intelligent hauntings to the spirits of deceased individuals who, for a variety of reasons, prefer to maintain their connection to the terrestrial world. It is possible that such hauntings are caused by a variety of factors, such as a wish to deliver a message, an unfinished business, or a reluctance to move on to the hereafter.

Phantoms of the Portals

The existence of "portals," which are regions where the curtain between dimensions is thin and therefore facilitates the occurrence of supernatural events, is a theory that is put up by some paranormal investigators and enthusiasts. During portal hauntings, it is possible for entities to enter and exit our reality with greater ease, which can result in an increase in the amount of paranormal activity in particular regions.

It is common for the idea of portals to have its origins in esoteric and metaphysical ideas. These beliefs claim that particular locations serve as doorways between various levels of existence. Despite the fact that this theory may not be supported by empirical evidence, it continues to be a topic of discussion in conversations regarding severe and persistent paranormal activity.

Variations in Ghostly Manifestations Across Different Cultures

Spirits belonging to ancestors in Asian cultures

The adoration of one's ancestors is extremely deeply rooted in the spiritual traditions of many Asian societies. One of the most important aspects of the cultural worldview is the concept of ancestral spirits, which are thought to keep a watchful eye on and direct their living descendants. It is possible for these spirits to present themselves in the form of dreams, apparitions, or even the feeling of a guardian presence.

Offerings and ceremonies are examples of the types of rituals that are related with ancestor veneration. These rituals are aimed to establish and preserve peace between the living and the dead. It is a cultural understanding of an ongoing connection between the living and the dead that is reflected in the concept of ancestral spirits.

The Yokai in the Folklore of Japan

The supernatural beings known as yokai, which are prevalent in Japanese folklore, include a vast variety of apparitions, monsters, and spirits. Yokai are a key component of Japanese culture. Yokai can be either benevolent or malicious, with some being mischievous and others being benevolent. The yurei, also known as ghostly spirits, are a prevalent motif in Japanese ghost stories. These stories are frequently associated with tragic or vindictive narratives.

As a result of the fact that these entities are woven into the fabric of literature, art, and traditions, the cultural significance of yokai goes beyond the realm of simple superstition at this point. A nuanced perspective on the supernatural is contributed to by the fact that they serve as both cautionary symbols and sources of inspiration.

Spirits and Faeries of the Celtic Tradition

The traditions of faeries, spirits, and other supernatural beings are deeply ingrained in the mythology and folklore of the Celtic people. The concept of the "sidhe," sometimes known as fairy folk, is widespread in Celtic legends. Interactions with these beings are frequently depicted as being both alluring and dangerous. There are certain landscapes that are thought to be sites where the veil between worlds is thin. Some examples of these landscapes include fairy rings and ancient burial mounds.

Faith in the spirits of nature, elemental forces, and otherworldly regions is a significant factor in the complex tapestry of spectral manifestations that are associated with Celtic culture. One of the recurrent themes that can be found in Celtic cultural narratives is the connectivity that exists between the natural and supernatural worlds.

Perspectives from the Scientific Community on Ghostly Manifestations

Aspects of Pathogenicity

Those who are skeptical of ghostly phenomena and certain researchers have proposed psychogenic explanations for them. The influence of the mind on perception is referred to as psychogenic elements, and it is common practice to attribute paranormal encounters to psychological and neurological events. There are a number of reasons that may lead to the impression of ghostly events. These include abnormalities in brain function, stress, suggestibility, and the power of suggestion.

For instance, the sensation of being watched, which is frequently reported in haunted sites, may be associated with heightened states of awareness or suggestibility. Visual manifestations of apparitions could also be explained by the phenomena known as "pareidolia," which occurs when the brain recognizes familiar patterns in stimuli that are completely dissimilar to one another.

Electromagnetic Fields and the Influence of environmental Elements

In the course of scientific research into haunted locales, the measuring of electromagnetic fields (EMF) and ambient elements is frequently carried out. The human brain may be influenced by variations in electromagnetic fields, according to the hypothesis of some experts. This could result in changed perceptions and experiences associated with haunted locales.

It has also been proposed that environmental elements, like infrasound, which is beyond the threshold of human hearing, could be potential contributors to the emergence of ghostly phenomena. It has been established that infrasound is associated with emotions of unease and discomfort, and the presence of infrasound in particular surroundings may have an effect on how one perceives paranormal occurrences.

Consciousness and Quantum Mechanics: Explanations

It has been suggested that the secrets of quantum physics have been evoked in order to provide an explanation for paranormal occurrences, as was discussed in the investigation of the junction of science and the supernatural.

It is the contention of those who hold this viewpoint that the nature of consciousness might be a factor in the formation of reality, and that quantum entanglement might make it easier for living people to communicate with those who have passed away.

Note, however, that such interpretations of quantum mechanics continue to be speculative and are not universally accepted within the scientific community. This is an extremely important point to keep in mind. There is a lack of unanimity among physicists and researchers on the applicability of quantum principles to consciousness and paranormal occurrences, despite the fact that this is a field that is consistently being investigated.

Methodologies and apparatus associated with the investigation and research of the paranormal

In order to investigate ghostly manifestations and haunting patterns, investigations into the paranormal make use of a wide variety of approaches and pieces of technology. Meters that measure electromagnetic fields (EMF), cameras that capture infrared light, audio recorders that record electronic voice phenomena (EVP), and motion sensors are all examples of common instruments. Measurement of environmental conditions and the collection of possible evidence of paranormal activity are both accomplished with the use of these instruments.

When conducting investigations, it is common practice to conduct interviews with witnesses in order to get first-hand accounts of events. It is also an essential component of paranormal investigations to conduct historical research on the background of a location, including the people who have lived there in the past and significant events that have occurred there.

Obstacles and Criticisms to Consider

Investigations into the paranormal are met with major obstacles and objections, which come from both within and outside of the international scientific community. Skeptics contend that a significant number of paranormal investigators lack scientific rigor and instead rely on personal encounters and anecdotal evidence with their findings. There are a number of factors that can undermine the credibility of paranormal research, including the absence of defined techniques and the possibility of bias in the interpretation of findings.

Furthermore, the influence of popular media, which is rife with sensationalized depictions of paranormal activity, has the potential to mold the opinions of the general public and to have an effect on the objectivity of investigations. In order to strengthen the credibility of paranormal research, there are investigators who stress the significance of adhering to scientific principles and working in conjunction with specialists in subjects that are pertinent to the investigation.

Regarding the Ethical Implications of Research on the Paranormal
Regard for the Beliefs of Other Cultures

When it comes to conducting research on the paranormal, it is of the utmost importance to respect cultural beliefs and sensitivities. A significant number of haunted places are connected to certain cultural narratives, historical events, or spiritual sites. In order to conduct investigations with cultural awareness, researchers need to take into consideration the potential impact that their study could have on the communities that are related with the regions they are investigating.

Consent and Confidentiality

When conducting investigations into the paranormal, it is common practice to visit private dwellings or historically significant locations. It is of the utmost importance to not only seek authorization to conduct investigations but also to respect the privacy and consent of property owners. In situations in which persons may be vulnerable or distressed as a result of having paranormal experiences, ethical considerations need an attitude that is empathetic and supportive.

Communication of the Results in a Responsible Manner

The integrity of paranormal research must be preserved at all costs, and responsible communication of findings is important to this pursuit. Those conducting the investigation ought to provide the evidence in an open and honest manner, taking into account any doubts and possible alternative explanations. Exaggeration and sensationalism have the potential to undermine the credibility of the field and contribute to the proliferation of public misunderstandings regarding the characteristics of paranormal occurrences.

A voyage into the heart of the unseen realm is a journey into the exploration of ghostly manifestations and haunting patterns. This is a domain that is intertwined with the threads of human experience, cultural beliefs, and the mysteries that resist easy explanation. The ongoing fascination with the supernatural, which is a reflection of our insatiable curiosity about the unknown, may be traced back to ancient folklore and continues throughout current inquiries.

In order to successfully navigate this area, it is vital that we approach the topic with a balance of open-minded curiosity and critical inquiry. Whether they are explained by psychogenic variables, environmental effects, or philosophical interpretations, ghostly manifestations provide a look into the intricate relationship that exists between the visible and the invisible.

The field of paranormal investigation is constantly evolving, despite the fact that it is confronted with obstacles and mistrust. In order to strengthen the legitimacy of their work, some investigators are using scientific procedures. In the stories of well-known hauntings, such as the Enfield Poltergeist or the Bell Witch haunting, we are presented with touchstones that encourage us to contemplate the riddles of existence and the enduring nature of awareness beyond the confines of life.

In the end, the investigation of ghostly manifestations is not only a search for evidence or confirmation; rather, it is an investigation of the human spirit and the enduring link it has to the mysteries of existence. We are guided by the threads of history, culture, and the everlasting human search to uncover the mysteries of the unseen as we make our way through the realms of the paranormal. As we do so, we tiptoe delicately on the threshold between the known and the unknown.

2.1 Classifying Ghosts: Residual vs. Intelligent hauntings

There is a wide variety of ghostly manifestations that fall under the umbrella of the world of paranormal phenomena. Each of these manifestations has its own set of qualities and ramifications. Remaining hauntings and intelligent hauntings are the two fundamental types that stand out among the many other classifications of hauntings which are available. The purpose of this investigation is to investigate the differences that exist between these classifications by analyzing the characteristics that define them, the cultural differences that make them unique, and the scientific viewpoints that add to our comprehension of these unexplained encounters with the supernatural.

Determining the Meaning of Residual Hauntings and Their Characteristics

Residents frequently refer to residual hauntings as psychic impressions that have been left on the environment. These imprints are said to replay particular events or feelings that are associated with a particular spot. Remainders of hauntings, in contrast to intelligent hauntings, do not involve any contact or awareness. It appears as though the energy or imprint is stuck in a never-ending loop, and it appears as though the events of the past are coming back to life.

Repetition: The haunting exhibits a repetitive quality, frequently reenacting a particular scene or event again and again.

Remaining hauntings are characterized by the fact that the entities involved are unaware of the living and do not engage in any kind of interaction with them.

Restricted to Particular Locations: Residual hauntings are frequently confined to specific locations, which are the locations where the traumatic or emotional events that transpired occurred.

Extreme emotional energy, which often originates from painful or highly charged experiences, is associated with these hauntings. These hauntings are linked to extreme emotional energy.

Possible explanations and hypotheses

According to the Stone Tape Theory, the environment has the ability to record or "store" prior experiences in a manner that is analogous to that of a tape recording. Under particular circumstances, it is possible that certain materials, such as stone, have the capacity to store energy and then release it to the environment.

Psychic Imprints: There are others who believe in the presence of psychic imprints from extreme emotional events. These individuals are known as paranormal enthusiasts. There is a possibility that these imprints will become imprinted on the environment and will occasionally reflect back under specific conditions.

Time-Slip Phenomena: There is a possibility that residual hauntings are connected to time-slip phenomena, which are situations in which people temporarily perceive events from the past or the future as a result of disruptions in the interplay between space and time.

Various Cultural Perspectives Regarding Hauntings That Remain

The perception and interpretation of residual hauntings are influenced by the cultural beliefs of the people. It is possible that residual hauntings are a manifestation of the spiritual energy that is embedded in the environment in cultures that have deep links to the spirits of their ancestors or the spirits of nature. The concept of a location that preserves the reverberations of events that occurred in the past is consistent with cultural narratives that place an emphasis on the connectivity of the tangible and the spiritual realms.

In many indigenous belief systems, particular areas are regarded as sacred, and residual hauntings may be interpreted as manifestations of the presence of spirits or as messages from the ancestors. These phenomena are frequently endowed with symbolic value and the belief in the continuation of spiritual forces is strengthened as a result of the cultural background, which molds the perception of these phenomena.

Definition and Characteristics of Hauntings Caused by Intelligent Beings

Intelligent hauntings are characterized by the presence of beings that give the impression of having self-awareness, consciousness, and the capacity to communicate with live people. Intelligent hauntings, in contrast to residual hauntings, frequently involve a degree of reactivity, in which spirits may converse with one another, control their surroundings, or display actions that are intended to accomplish a specific goal.

Interaction: Entities who are responsible for intelligent hauntings have the ability to communicate with live people through a variety of interactions, including communication, the movement of things, or direct physical contact.

Behaviors that are indicative of intentionality are exhibited by the entities. These behaviors include the transmission of messages, the pursuit of attention, and the implementation of responses to inputs.

Aware of their surroundings, intelligent creatures exhibit awareness of their environment and may realize the presence of living individuals.

There are many different manifestations that can occur as a result of intelligent hauntings. These manifestations include audible occurrences, visual apparitions, and the manipulation of the physical surroundings.

Possible explanations and hypotheses

The concept of survival after death is based on the idea that the consciousness or spirit of a person who has passed away continues to exist after their physical death, enabling them to continue to interact with those who are still alive.

Unresolved Business: It is possible that entities that are the subject of intelligent hauntings are considered to have unfinished business or wants that have not been satisfied, which compels them to maintain their connection to the realm of the mortals.

Some people believe that live people have the ability to project their ideas, feelings, or consciousness, producing apparitions that appear to be intelligent entities. This phenomenon is known as energetic projection.

Understanding Intelligent Hauntings from a Cultural Perspective

Individuals' conceptions of intelligent hauntings are heavily influenced by their cultural beliefs. It is possible that experiences with intelligent entities are seen as visits from deceased loved ones who are imparting instruction or protection in societies where ancestor veneration is popular. Within the context of cultural frameworks, the way in which these experiences are perceived is influenced by the belief in a hereafter as well as the continuity of consciousness.

Intelligent hauntings may be seen as possibilities for engagement with the spirit world in different cultures, particularly those that have a long history of communicating with spirits. In order to encourage communication with the entities, rituals, ceremonies, or mediums may be utilized. This will allow for a reciprocal interaction to exist between the living and the deceased.

Perspectives from the Scientific Community on Ghostly Manifestations
Definitions of Psychogenic Factors

When seen from a scientific perspective, psychogenic explanations postulate that both residual and intelligent hauntings are the result of the human mind and perception. The perception of ghostly occurrences may be influenced by a number of factors, including psychological stress, suggestibility, and cognitive biases.

It is possible that psychogenic variables are responsible for residual hauntings, which are characterized by a feeling of reliving past events or experiencing a psychic imprint. It is possible that psychological factors can impact the interpretation of ambiguous stimuli in intelligent hauntings, which can then lead to the experience of purposeful interaction with entities.

Variables in the Environment

Environmental elements, such as electromagnetic fields (EMF) and infrasound, have been investigated as possible contributors to the occurrence of ghostly manifestations. Alterations in electromagnetic fields (EMF), which can be caused by natural phenomena or by sources created by humans, have the potential to influence brain activity and contribute to altered perceptions. Infrasound, which is beyond the threshold of human hearing, has been linked to sensations of dread and discomfort, and it may have the potential to influence how people perceive paranormal occurrences.

Although it is possible that these environmental factors play a part in the formation of ghostly experiences, the relationship between these factors and particular hauntings continues to be complicated and difficult to define.

Consciousness and Quantum Mechanics: Explanations

It has been suggested that the interaction of quantum mechanics and consciousness can provide an explanation for a variety of paranormal events, including manifestations of ghosts. The proponents of this viewpoint propose that the nature of consciousness may have the ability to alter the activity of subatomic particles, which would make it easier for living people to interact with those who have passed away.

However, it is essential to keep in mind that the application of quantum concepts to consciousness and other paranormal occurrences is a highly speculative endeavor that is not widely accepted within the scientific community. There are several obstacles to overcome in order to establish a conclusive connection between these events, including the intricacies of quantum mechanics and the absence of empirical data connecting them.

Investigating Hauntings While Keeping Ethical Considerations in Mind

Honor and reverence for the Slain

When conducting investigations into the paranormal, especially those that involve intelligent hauntings, it is of the utmost importance to show respect for the deceased. In order to determine whether or not the entities exist, investigators need to approach them with care and empathy, taking into account the possibility that these beings have consciousness and agency.

Assent and Confidentiality

Those who conduct paranormal investigations and visit private dwellings or historically significant locations are required to acquire permission from the owners of the property and to respect their right to privacy. When dealing with situations in which humans may be distressed by paranormal events, it is necessary to handle the situation with compassion and assistance because of ethical reasons.

Communication of the Results in a Responsible Manner

The conclusions of the investigation should be communicated in a responsible manner by the investigators, who should also present the evidence openly and acknowledge any uncertainties. The potential influence that investigations could have on the reputations of individuals, historical locations, or cultural narratives necessitates a commitment to the distribution of facts in a responsible and ethical manner.

A framework that allows for a better understanding of the varied nature of paranormal events is provided by the classification of ghosts into two categories: residual hauntings and intelligent hauntings.

A psychic imprint that has been left on the surroundings is suggested by residual hauntings due to the fact that they are repeated and do not involve any interaction. Ghosts that are intelligent, on the other hand, involve beings that give the impression of being self-aware and are able to communicate with living people in a purposeful manner.

Beliefs in the afterlife, ancestor spirits, and spirit contact all play a role in shaping cultural narratives, which further contribute to the enormous impact that cultural viewpoints have on the interpretation of these hauntings. Psychogenic elements, environmental influences, or hypothetical ties to quantum physics and consciousness are frequently the focal points of explanations in the scientific community.

In order to successfully navigate the domain of ghostly manifestations that cannot be seen, it is vital to approach the topic with a balanced viewpoint, taking into consideration the wealth of cultural beliefs as well as the insights that can be gained from scientific investigation. We are prompted to contemplate the riddles of existence, the nature of awareness, and the unbreakable connection that exists between the living and the dead as we investigate residual and intelligent hauntings. In the course of this ongoing investigation, the threads of history, culture, and human curiosity are woven together in order to discover the mysteries of the unseen.

2.2 Examining Common Phenomena: Apparitions, poltergeists, and more

Throughout the years, the domain of the paranormal has been a source of fascination and bafflement for people. It has given rise to a multitude of occurrences that cannot be explained, which in turn challenges our understanding of the natural world. When it comes to these mysterious phenomena, apparitions and poltergeists stand out as some of the most fascinating and perplexing experiences that people from a variety of cultures and time periods have reported having. In the course of this investigation, we delve into the nature of these events, making an effort to solve the mysteries that surround them and investigating the scientific and cultural perspectives that strive to explain or dismiss them.

The Apparitions: Encounters with the Ghosts

The apparition, which is typically characterized as the appearance of a ghost or spirit, is one of the paranormal phenomena that has received the greatest attention from the media. There have been several reports of these ghostly entities being described as forms that are translucent or semi-transparent, and they sometimes resemble people who have passed away. There are many different environments that are connected with apparitions, such as haunted houses, historic sites, and even everyday areas. Skeptics believe that such sightings are the result of hallucinations, psychological causes, or the power of suggestion. On the other hand, believers contend that these encounters provide evidence of an afterlife or a realm that is beyond our comprehension.

Several eyewitness stories of apparitions describe encounters that elicit feelings of dread, amazement, or melancholy in the individuals who witnessed them. There are many who assert that they have had the opportunity to converse with these apparitions, recounting stories of messages from the hereafter or unfinished business that keeps the spirits bound to the realm of the living. These apparitions have left an unmistakable impression on the collective memory of communities all across the world, from the Lady in White who haunts historic castles to the ghostly soldiers who fight on battlefields.

Poltergeists, often known as the Spirits of Mischief

In addition to apparitions, the poltergeist is another typical type of paranormal activity that people experience. "Poltergeist" is a term that originates from the German terms "poltern," which means to produce noise, and "geist," which means spirit. In contrast to the typical apparitions of ghosts, poltergeists are characterized by their disruptive activity and their capacity to exert influence over the surrounding physical world. Some of the most common occurrences that are related with poltergeist activity are sounds that cannot be explained, items that move, and even physical assaults conducted against persons.

Incidents involving poltergeists frequently revolve around a particular person, who is referred to as the "focus" or "agent." The disruptive phenomena are thought to be the result of the agent's unconscious generation of psychokinetic energy, which presents itself in the form of events. One school of thought contends that poltergeist activity can be traced back to natural origins, such as infrasound or electromagnetic forces, while another school of thought considers it to be manifestations of suppressed emotions or psychokinetic powers.

Different Points of View, Scientific and Skeptical

When it comes to the scientific method, the investigation of supernatural occurrences is fraught with a great deal of difficulty. When it comes to the investigation of ghosts, apparitions, and poltergeists, it is challenging to apply conventional scientific procedures due to the absence of factual data, the subjective character of personal experiences, and the impossibility to reproduce such occurrences under controlled settings.

Dismissing paranormal encounters as the result of imagination, suggestibility, or cognitive biases is a common practice among the skeptical community. A number of psychological causes, including sleep paralysis and hypnagogic hallucinations, are widely mentioned as potential explanations for apparitions. In the same vein, poltergeist activity might be linked to environmental circumstances, hoaxes, or the subconscious activities of the individuals who are engaged.

Believers contend that dismissing paranormal experiences entirely is a reductionist approach that misses the variety of human experience. This is despite the fact that these skeptical perspectives exist. They place a strong emphasis on the significance of anecdotal evidence and the cultural meaning of these phenomena, implying that there may be aspects of the cosmos that science has not yet fully comprehended.

Discussions of Folklore and Cultural Perspectives

The ubiquity of poltergeists and apparitions in folklore and cultural traditions is another factor that contributes to the complexity of these phenomena. Stories of ghostly encounters are woven into the fabric of oral traditions in a variety of different countries. These stories are then passed down from generation to generation of people. The objective of these cultural narratives is frequently multifaceted, ranging from providing explanations for things that cannot be explained to imparting moral lessons or enforcing societal standards.

For instance, in Japanese legend, the yūrei are vengeful spirits that are thought to possess the ability to return from the afterlife in order to seek retribution. In a similar vein, the Celtic tradition makes reference to banshees, which are supernatural beings whose cries indicate that death is on the horizon. These cultural interpretations shed light on the myriad of approaches that societies have taken in order to engage with the unknown and incorporate paranormal experiences into their collective awareness.

The Function of Technology in the Investigation of Paranormal Occurrences

New instruments have been made available to paranormal investigators as a result of technological advancements, which have enabled them to document and examine purported supernatural phenomena. Paranormal investigators, armed with infrared cameras, electromagnetic field meters, and audio recording equipment, are on the lookout for proof of apparitions and poltergeists. Although there are those who contend that the use of such technology has provided paranormal investigations with a certain degree of credibility, there are also those who question the absence of defined techniques and the possibility of these investigations being misinterpreted.

The usage of electronic voice phenomenon (EVP) recordings, for example, includes recording voices or noises that cannot be explained using audio technology. Audio pareidolia is a psychological phenomenon in which the human brain interprets random sounds as recognized patterns or phrases. Skeptics frequently ascribe these findings to audio pareidolia. The controversy around the dependability of technology evidence highlights the difficulties that arise when attempting to bridge the gap between the subjective experiences of humans and the objective scrutiny of the scientific community.

The bridge between science and the supernatural is known as parapsychology

A bridge between the realms of science and the supernatural is the goal of the scientific field of research known as parapsychology, which investigates phenomena that are considered to be supernatural. Proponents of parapsychological research claim that it can lead to a greater knowledge of consciousness, perception, and the potential interconnection of all living things. This is despite the fact that conventional science continues to be dubious about parapsychological research.

Research in the field of parapsychology involves a wide variety of phenomena, such as telekinesis, near-death experiences, and extrasensory perception (ESP). The goal of parapsychologists is to identify patterns and anomalies that may contradict the answers that are currently employed by the scientific community through the use of controlled experiments and statistical studies. On the other hand, the field is confronted with difficulties in terms of replication, finance, and the stigma that is traditionally associated with exploring the paranormal.

When typical paranormal occurrences like apparitions and poltergeists are investigated, a complex interaction of cultural, psychological, and scientific components is revealed. Believing individuals argue for the significance of personal experiences and the richness of cultural traditions that include these events into the human narrative. Skeptics, on the other hand, highlight the absence of empirical evidence and the influence of cognitive biases.

It is a reflection of the inherent tension that exists between subjective experiences and the rigorous standards of scientific investigation that the continuous debate surrounding the paranormal is a reflection of. The investigation of apparitions, poltergeists, and other unexplained occurrences is expected to continue as technology continues to progress and interdisciplinary study continues to be conducted. This will pose a challenge to our understanding of reality and the mysteries that lay beyond the confines of conventional knowledge.

Chapter 3

The Physics of the Unseen

The field of physics has, for a very long time, been committed to the task of elucidating the mysteries that surround the observable universe. Physicists have made tremendous progress in their understanding of the underlying laws that govern our existence, taking into account everything from subatomic particles to the great expanses of space. Nevertheless, there is a vast region that is beyond the capabilities of our senses and equipment; this is the realm of the unseen. The purpose of this investigation is to investigate the physics of the unseen by investigating phenomena such as dark matter, dark energy, quantum entanglement, and the nature of consciousness. All of these phenomena present a challenge to our conventional understanding of the universe.

Dark matter is a mystery that cannot be seen

In the field of current physics, the nature of dark matter is considered to be one of the most profound mysteries. Despite the fact that it does not emit, absorb, or reflect light, dark matter is able to exert a gravitational influence on visible matter, which in turn affects the motion of galaxies and galaxy clusters. Dark matter is considered to be elusive because it is unable to be directly seen by traditional telescopes and other observational tools, despite the fact that it can be found everywhere and accounts for around 27 percent of the universe.

A number of other hypothetical particles, including weakly interacting massive particles (WIMPs) and axions, have been suggested as possible candidates for dark matter that could exist in the universe. Experiments are currently being conducted all over the world in an effort to indirectly detect these elusive particles by the interactions that they are theorized to have with regular matter. Researchers at facilities such as the Large Hadron Collider (LHC) are working toward the goal of producing and detecting dark matter particles in controlled laboratory environments. This research extends beyond the realms of astrophysics and cosmology, reaching into the world of particle physics.

The Accelerator of the Cosmic Process: Dark Energy

The cosmos comprises a number of unexplained components, one of which is dark energy, which is the counterpart to dark matter. The acceleration of the expansion of the universe is caused by dark energy, which, in contrast to dark matter, exerts a force that is repulsive. Despite the fact that it was first discovered through measurements of supernovae, dark energy continues to be one of the most important mysteries in contemporary physics.

The cosmological constant, which was first brought to light by Albert Einstein in his theory of general relativity, is currently the most prominent concept for dark energy. On the other hand, the disparity between the predictions of theory and the facts obtained from observations has resulted in continuous discussions and the investigation of alternative hypotheses, such as quintessence and modified gravity. It is essential to have a solid understanding of the nature of dark energy in order to discover the destiny of the universe, which will determine whether it will continue to expand indefinitely or eventually collapse.

Spooky action at a distance is what quantum entanglement is all about

Entanglement is a fascinating phenomenon that lays at the core of the foundation of quantum mechanics science. The quantum states of two particles become interdependent when they become entangled, regardless of the distance that separates them from one another or from one another. As a result of the fact that changes in the state of one particle instantly affect the state of the other, Einstein famously referred to entanglement as "spooky action at a distance."

Quantum entanglement presents a challenge to our traditional intuitions regarding the separability of objects that are relatively far away and the constraints that are imposed by the speed of light. Although there are numerous tests that demonstrate the existence of entanglement, the mechanism that underlies it continues to be a mystery. Quantum computing, quantum communication, and quantum teleportation are all areas of research that are now being conducted to take use of the one-of-a-kind qualities of entangled particles. The phenomenon may have practical ramifications.

A Bridge Between Philosophy and Physics: An Examination of the Nature of Consciousness

Moving beyond the worlds of the microscopic and the cosmic, the investigation of the unseen reaches into the secrets of consciousness. In both the field of physics and the field of philosophy, one of the most fundamental and enigmatic issues is posed by the nature of consciousness. This inquiry explores how the physical processes that occur in the brain give rise to subjective experience.

Neuroscientists do research on the neurological correlates of consciousness, with the goal of determining the exact brain activity that are connected with various characteristics of awareness. In the meantime, physicists are conducting research that spans multiple disciplines in order to investigate the possible connections that exist between the quantum realm and consciousness. It has been hypothesized, according to theories such as the orchestrated objective reduction (Orch-OR) theory, that quantum processes that occur within microtubules of neurons are responsible for the generation of consciousness.

The investigation of the connection between physics and consciousness welcomes a convergence of disciplines, which challenges the traditional boundaries that have been established between the sciences and the humanities. This is despite the fact that the topic of quantum consciousness continues to be a subject of speculation and controversy.

Increasing the Number of Dimensions Through String Theory and Multiverse Hypotheses

String theory is an ambitious attempt to unite the fundamental forces of nature. It does this by characterizing particles as "strings" that are one-dimensional and vibrate at different frequencies. In addition to the three spatial dimensions and one temporal dimension that are commonly known, this theory presents the idea of additional dimensions for consideration. On the other hand, these additional dimensions are compressed at scales that are too much smaller to be directly detected.

The notion of a multiverse, which is a huge collection of worlds with different physical constants and rules of nature, is an intriguing application of string theory that has implications that are exciting. The multiverse hypothesis is based on the concept that different compactifications of extra dimensions could result in the formation of universes that have different characteristics. It is possible that the multiverse provides an explanation for the fine-tuning of physical constants that have been seen in our world, despite the fact that it is still highly speculative.

Inflation of the Cosmic System: Moving from the Unseen to the Observable

The idea of cosmic inflation offers a strong framework for comprehending the structure of the universe on a massive scale, which can be observed. In order to provide an explanation for the homogeneity of the cosmic microwave background radiation and the large-scale structure of galaxies, the theory of cosmic inflation proposes that the universe experienced a brief period of rapid and exponential expansion in the early instances.

There are a number of observable mysteries that can be well answered by inflationary cosmology; however, the process that causes inflation has not yet been discovered. There is another aspect of the unseen in cosmology that is represented by the inflationary field that is responsible for the expansion. This field is frequently referred to as the inflaton. Inflationary models are being refined by physicists in order to correspond with the most recent observational evidence, and they are continuing their investigation into the features of the inflaton.

The Heisenberg Uncertainty Principle and Its Implications for the Limits of Observation

The Uncertainty Principle, which was developed by Werner Heisenberg, imposes a fundamental limitation on our capacity to simultaneously measure certain pairs of physical variables, such as position and momentum, with absolute precision.

This fundamental concept, which is a cornerstone of quantum mechanics, highlights the inherent restrictions that are imposed by the quantum nature of everything that exists.

The Uncertainty Principle proposed by Heisenberg suggests that there are features of the physical universe that are inherently uncertain and cannot be known. The simple act of observation causes a change in the state of the system that is being viewed, which highlights the inherent difficulties that are involved in investigating the components of the quantum realm that are not visible. The Uncertainty Principle is a philosophical concept that encourages contemplation on the nature of reality as well as the interaction that exists between the observer and the observed entities.

In the context of the quantum measurement problem, the role of conscious observation

Within the realm of quantum physics, the act of observing brings about an additional layer of complexity, which is known as the quantum measurement issue. In situations where a quantum system is in a state of superposition, the act of measuring causes the system to collapse into one of the potential states. The question of what exactly defines a "measurement" and how this measurement can lead to the collapse of the wave function is one that continues to be the subject of discussion and investigation.

There are a number of different interpretations of quantum physics, including the Copenhagen interpretation, the many-worlds interpretation, and the de Broglie-Bohm interpretation, all of which propose different solutions to the measurement problem. The nature of reality and the part that conscious perception plays in determining the results of quantum experiments are both understood differently by these interpretations, which offer unique viewpoints on the subject.

Beyond Dark Matter and Dark Energy lies the realm of dark physics

Even while dark matter and dark energy are the most common topics of conversation when it comes to the unseen in the universe, the idea of dark physics encompasses more than just these mysterious substances. The term "dark physics" refers to the more comprehensive endeavor of comprehending the fundamental nature of the universe, which includes components that are difficult to observe or quantify.

Unseen forces and particles are the subject of continuing research in the field of particle physics. Some examples of things that are being looked into include the possibility of sterile neutrinos or other foreign particles. In the event that these hypothetical entities are shown to exist, they have the potential to offer solutions to unanswered problems concerning the make-up of the universe and the characteristics of the fundamental forces.

The Unification of the Fundamental Forces Through Quantum Gravity

The search for a unified theory of quantum gravity is one of the most significant issues that theoretical physics is now currently facing. Because general relativity is incompatible with quantum physics on small scales, efforts have been made to build a unified framework. This is despite the fact that general relativity is able to successfully represent the force of gravity on large scales.

String theory, loop quantum gravity, and causal dynamical triangulations are some of the theories that are being investigated as part of the hunt for quantum gravity. By attempting to reconcile the discrete and granular nature of spacetime that is proposed by quantum mechanics with the smooth and continuous spacetime that is described by general relativity, these initiatives are designed to achieve their goal. In the event that this mission is accomplished, it would be a significant step toward achieving an all-encompassing comprehension of the fundamental forces that control the universe.

The investigation of the physics of the unseen reveals a complex web of mysteries that are intertwined with one another and go beyond the limits of our current comprehension. Physics is a field that grapples with topics that challenge our ideas of reality. These questions range from the mystery of consciousness to the forces that shape the universe that are not apparent to us. The unseen continues to lure humans, urging them to journey into unexplored territory and embrace the unknown. This invitation comes as technology continues to improve and theoretical frameworks continue to grow. The pursuit of the unseen is what motivates the continual voyage of discovery that characterizes the essence of physics. This might be accomplished through the investigation of dark matter and dark energy, or it might be accomplished through the search for a unified theory of everything.

3.1 Energy and Frequencies: Exploring the science behind apparitions

Encounters with ghosts, which are frequently coupled with the phenomenon of apparitions, have been a source of fascination and confusion for people over the course of history. The realms of energy and vibrations are investigated in a scientific investigation of apparitions, in contrast to the numerous cultural and spiritual explanations that are available. By attempting to understand how the interaction of energy fields and frequencies could contribute to the perception and manifestation of apparitions, this investigation tries to challenge the conventional boundaries that have been established between the seen and the unseen.

The Human Body's Source of Energy

It is vital to begin by investigating the energy that is present within the human body in order to gain an understanding of the scientific foundations that underpin apparitions.

All of the biochemical and bioelectrical activities that occur within the human body are intricately intertwined with one another. One of the many physiological functions that involves the generation and transfer of energy is the firing of neurons in the brain. Other physiological functions include the pounding of the heart.

Bioelectromagnetic energy, which is generated by the electrical activity of cells and tissues, is an essential component. Particularly abundant sources of bioelectromagnetic fields are found in the cardiovascular system, the brain, and the neurological system. The electromagnetic aura that is produced by these forces extends beyond the body and can be detected and quantified by instruments that are sensitive to electro-magnetic fields.

The Brain and the Effects of Electromagnetic Fields

Intricate electrochemical processes are responsible for the functioning of the brain, which is sometimes regarded as the epicenter of consciousness. In order to interact with one another, neurons send electrical impulses, which results in the formation of electromagnetic fields. Not only do these fields extend beyond the confines of the brain, but they also extend into the area around it.

Alterations in the electromagnetic fields of the brain may be connected with altered states of consciousness, including those that are associated with paranormal experiences, according to research that has been conducted that shows this correlation. The scientific examination into the paranormal includes a large component that focuses on the study of these brainwave patterns and how they are connected to apparitional encounters.

The Use of Frequencies and Resonance

It is essential to have a solid grasp of resonance, which is the phenomena in which a system vibrates in response to an external force, in order to comprehend the ways in which energy and frequencies could be involved in the perception of apparitions. At a natural frequency, everything, including the human body, vibrates. This frequency is known as the natural frequency. The resonance that takes place as a result of being exposed to external stimuli that match this natural frequency amplifies the vibrations occurring.

Regarding the phenomenon of apparitions, it is feasible that particular surroundings or conditions could generate resonance with the bioelectromagnetic fields of individuals, so enhancing or modifying their sense of reality. According to this theory of resonance, apparitions could be experienced by individuals when they come into contact with particular energy fields or frequencies that resonate with their own bioelectromagnetic fingerprints. This hypothesis implies that apparitions could be experienced through a possible process.

In the field of quantum physics, non-locality

There is also a connection between the investigation of apparitions and the principles of quantum physics, namely the phenomenon of non-locality among these concepts. The ability of particles to have immediate connections with one another, regardless of the distance that separates them, is referred to as non-locality. Quantum entanglement has been used to establish experimentally that this breach of classical ideas of locality has occurred.

If the consciousness or energy that is linked with persons possesses quantum features, then the non-local nature of quantum phenomena might provide a framework for understanding how apparitions might express themselves. Entanglement in quantum mechanics hints at the notion of a possible interconnection that is not constrained by spatial boundaries. This opens the door to the possibility of non-local communication or perception possibilities.

The Importance of Environmental Characteristics

There are a number of environmental components that contribute to the overall energy landscape in which apparitional experiences take place. These aspects include electromagnetic fields, geophysical processes, and atmospheric and atmospheric conditions. Some academics believe that particular environmental conditions may play a role in triggering or amplifying apparitional encounters. Certain sites are known for being "haunted," and some experts believe that these factors may play a role.

A number of geophysical abnormalities, including fluctuations in the magnetic field of the Earth, have been demonstrated to be connected with paranormal experiences. It is also possible that the experience of apparitions could be affected by the presence of high levels of electromagnetic fields in particular surroundings, regardless of whether these fields are natural or constructed by humans. The goal of the investigations that are being conducted to determine the association between environmental elements and reported apparitional activity is to discover patterns that could possibly explain the predominance of situations like this in specific locales.

The frequencies of infrasound and subsonic waves

Infrasound, which refers to sound waves that are below the threshold of human hearing, has been proposed as an additional possible factor that contributes to apparitional experiences. It has been demonstrated through research that being exposed to infrasound can cause certain persons to experience emotions of discomfort, anxiety, and even hallucinations. Consequently, this has led to the suggestion that infrasound, which can be produced by either natural or manmade sources, might be the cause of some of the apparitional encounters that have been observed.

Furthermore, subsonic frequencies, which are frequencies that are beyond the range of audible sound, may potentially play a role in the formation of perceptual perceptions. It is possible that these low-frequency vibrations could have an effect on the human sensory system, which could result in the perception of apparitions or other paranormal events. The investigation of infrasound and subsonic frequencies sheds information on the complex nature of environmental elements that may play a role in the scientific explanation of apparitions.

Perspectives from the fields of psychology and neuroscience

In spite of the fact that the investigation of energy and frequencies offers a scientific perspective from which to investigate apparitions, it is of the utmost importance to acknowledge the psychological and neurological aspects of these experiences. An essential component in the formation of perceptions is the human mind, which is shaped by a variety of factors including beliefs, feelings, and cognitive processes.

The interpretation of paranormal experiences, such as apparitions, is frequently up to individual interpretation and is impacted by a variety of elements, including cultural, social, and personal aspects. It is possible for psychological mechanisms to have a role in the formation of apparitional experiences. Some examples of these mechanisms include suggestibility and pareidolia, which is the tendency to recognize familiar patterns in an otherwise random stimulus.

There is a possibility that the perception of apparitions is also influenced by neurological conditions. These elements include altered states of consciousness, sleep paralysis, and neurological illnesses. For a thorough investigation into the scientific underpinnings of apparitions, it is essential to have a solid understanding of the reciprocal relationship that exists between psychological and neurological components, as well as the postulated energy and frequency-based mechanisms.

Instrumentation and Emerging Technologies currently in use

The scientific investigation of apparitions has had new opportunities made available to it as a result of developments in technology and instruments. Researchers have the ability to quantify and study the energy and environmental conditions that are connected with claimed paranormal experiences by utilizing specialized equipment such as electromagnetic field meters, thermal cameras, and environmental sensors.

In addition, breakthroughs in neuroimaging techniques have provided insights into the brain correlates of experiences that are considered to be abnormal. Researchers are able to detect brain activity during claimed apparitional experiences through the use of functional magnetic resonance imaging (fMRI) and electroencephalography (EEG), which helps shed insight on the neuronal mechanisms that are involved.

An activity that encompasses multiple dimensions is the investigation of the scientific principles that underlie apparitions via the lenses of energy and frequency. The search for an understanding of the mechanisms that underlie apparitional experiences is a complicated and linked endeavor. These mechanisms include the bioelectromagnetic fields that exist within the human body, environmental influences, resonance, and quantum principles.

It is vital to approach the study of apparitions with a comprehensive perspective that covers psychological, neurological, and cultural components. This is because scientific research can provide useful insights; but, it is also not enough to just investigate apparitions. It is possible that the convergence of various fields of study, in conjunction with the incorporation of developing technologies, may be able to solve the mysteries surrounding apparitions and offer a more nuanced comprehension of the dynamic interaction that exists between the realms that can be seen and those that cannot be seen.

3.2 Quantum Entanglement: How it may relate to ghostly encounters

Quantum entanglement, a phenomena that Albert Einstein famously referred to as "spooky action at a distance," is an essential ingredient in the field of quantum mechanics. Although it was initially investigated in the field of particle physics, the unexplained and instantaneous connection between entangled particles has prompted intriguing theories about its potential significance to phenomena that extend beyond the domain of the microscopic. The purpose of this investigation is to bridge the gap between the realms of quantum physics and the supernatural by delving into the idea of quantum entanglement and investigating the potential connections that exist between quantum entanglement and ghostly encounters.

Entanglement in Quantum Systems: A Concise Introduction

The concept of superposition, which enables particles to exist in several states at the same time, is the fundamental idea that underpins quantum entanglement. Entanglement occurs when two or more particles become entangled with one another, causing their states to become entwined. This means that the qualities of one particle immediately affect the properties of the other particle, regardless of the distance that separates them.

The violation of Bell inequalities is the most notable example of the experimental validation of the entanglement of particles, which has been demonstrated through a multitude of investigations. Quantum entanglement is a phenomenon that has been demonstrated to be a robust and persistent feature of the quantum universe. This phenomenon challenges conventional intuitions about the separability of distant objects, despite the fact that the physics underlying quantum entanglement remain as obscure as ever.

As well as Non-Locality and Quantum States

During the entangled state, the quantum properties of one particle, such as spin or polarization, become correlated with the properties of the other particle. This occurs when the two particles are in two different states. The instantaneous determination of the state of the entangled partner can be made by measuring the state of a single particle, even if the entangled partner is located light-years distant. Due to the fact that changes to a single particle appear to take place at a rate that is faster than the speed of light, this non-local connection presents a challenge to our traditional ideas of causality and locality.

However, the nature of this non-local connection continues to be one of the parts of quantum physics that is the most difficult to understand. The method by which information is conveyed between entangled particles defies a straightforward explanation within the framework of classical physics. This is despite the fact that the effects of entanglement have been well-established.

It is hypothesized that quantum entanglement and ghostly encounters are occurring

It is the notion that consciousness or energy linked with persons might display quantum qualities, which would allow for non-local interactions that are comparable to entanglement. This concept is the source of the connection between quantum entanglement and ghostly encounters. A number of speculative hypotheses investigate the possibility that quantum entanglement is connected to paranormal encounters, including the following:

Consciousness at the Quantum Level: The proponents of the quantum consciousness hypothesis believe that the phenomenon of consciousness itself is entangled at a quantum level. Quantum qualities may be exhibited by the neuronal processes of the brain, particularly those processes that are involved in the generation of conscious experiences, according to this suggestion. One possible interpretation of this is that it suggests a non-local connection that goes beyond the conventional understanding of how the brain works.

Another theory suggests that quantum interactions with the environment, such as fluctuations in the magnetic field of the Earth or other quantum-scale phenomena, may play a part in the manifestation of ghostly encounters. This hypothesis is based on the idea that quantum interactions may play a role in the manifestation of ghostly encounters. In this setting, individuals have the potential to become entangled with their surroundings, which would provide a foundation for experiences that are not typical.

Quantum Entanglement and Energy Residue: There are others who believe that the emotional energy or leftover energy that is associated with traumatic experiences may become entangled with a certain area.

It is possible that this energy residue will remain and continue to impact the perception of persons who come into contact with it, which may result in the occurrence of ghostly encounters.

Complications and Criticisms Regarding the Theory

Quantum systems are extremely vulnerable to decoherence, which is the process by which entangled particles lose their quantum correlations while interacting with the external environment. Quantum systems are particularly susceptible to decoherence. One school of thought contends that the fragile nature of quantum states makes it difficult for macroscopic biological systems, such as the human brain, to keep coherent quantum states that are relevant to entanglement.

Discrepancies in size: The size at which quantum effects normally occur is substantially different from the scale at which ordinary experiences are experienced. Despite the fact that quantum entanglement has been demonstrated at the microscopic level, the application of these principles to macroscopic entities, such as human consciousness, creates obstacles that are related to scale disparities.

Debate Regarding the Quantum Nature of Consciousness The concept that consciousness itself possesses quantum qualities is one that is extensively disputed among the scientific world. Regarding the relevance of quantum phenomena to cognitive processes, the majority of neuroscientists and cognitive scientists subscribe to classical models of brain function and consciousness. This raises doubt regarding the possibility of quantum phenomena being applied to cognitive processes.

Dearth of Empirical Evidence There is a dearth of empirical evidence about the connection between quantum entanglement and ghostly encounters. Anecdotal claims of paranormal encounters certainly exist; nevertheless, in order to prove a causal link to quantum entanglement, serious scientific inquiry and validation are required.

Quantum parapsychology and empirical investigations:

In spite of the difficulties that arise from the theoretical framework, there are academics that call for empirical investigations into the possible connections that exist between quantum entanglement and paranormal observations. The study of paranormal experiences, such as ghostly encounters, is the focus of the field of quantum parapsychology, which aims to apply the principles of quantum mechanics to the investigation of these experiences.

Quantum states or phenomena are frequently measured in experimental designs, and these measurements are typically carried out in situations that are related with claimed psychic activity. Researchers might, for instance, investigate whether or if there is a correlation between fluctuations in quantum fields, such as magnetic fields or photon emissions, and the fact that ghostly encounters have been observed. While admitting the theoretical nature of such endeavors, the purpose of these investigations is to bridge the gap between quantum theory and observed occurrences.

Considerations of an Ethical Nature and the Intersection of Different Disciplines

There are ethical questions and challenges that arise at the junction of physics, psychology, and parapsychology as a result of the investigation of quantum entanglement and its putative relevance to ghostly encounters. An approach that is nuanced is required in order to strike a balance between the need for scientific rigor and respect for persons who report having paranormal experiences.

It is necessary for researchers to maintain a balance between the objective nature of scientific investigation and the subjective nature of personal testimonies. When it comes to the potential consequences of study findings, ethical problems also extend to the interpretations that link quantum phenomena to paranormal experiences. These interpretations have the ability to influence public views and beliefs.

Exploration of quantum entanglement and its possible significance to ghostly experiences is placed at the crossroads of physics, consciousness studies, and parapsychology. This intersection is where the discoveries are being made. The goal of comprehending the interwoven realms of quantum physics and the paranormal continues to fascinate the imagination of researchers as well as enthusiasts, despite the fact that there are several theoretical hurdles and objections.

The hypothesis that quantum entanglement is linked to ghostly encounters is a speculative one, which highlights the importance of conducting meticulous scientific research and validating the hypothesis through empirical evidence. The research of these interconnected realms may provide insights that question our understanding of consciousness, reality, and the unseen forces that may impact our experiences of the paranormal. This may be the case as technology continues to improve and as interdisciplinary collaboration becomes more in-depth.

3.3 Electromagnetic Fields: Investigating their role in hauntings

Electromagnetic fields (EMFs) have emerged as a main point of inquiry in light of the fact that the investigation of paranormal occurrences frequently includes digging into the enigmatic and inexplicable. As a result of the fact that reports of hauntings and ghostly encounters usually correlate with changes in electromagnetic activity, researchers have begun to investigate the possibility of a connection between electromagnetic fields and paranormal experiences. In this analysis, we dig into the characteristics of electromagnetic fields, the origins of these fields, and the scientific investigations that are being conducted to determine the role that electromagnetic fields play in hauntings.

Acquiring Knowledge of Electromagnetic Field Types

One of the most fundamental aspects of physics is the concept of electromagnetic fields, which encompass the interaction between electricity and magnetic forces. This is because these fields are produced anytime an electric charge is in motion, which results in the creation of waves that travel through space. Extremely low-frequency (ELF) waves, radio waves, microwaves, infrared, visible light, ultraviolet, X-rays, and gamma rays are all included in the electromagnetic spectrum. This spectrum encompasses a wide variety of frequencies.

In the context of inquiries into the paranormal, the lower end of the electromagnetic spectrum, in particular electromagnetic low frequency (ELF) waves and the potential influence that they could have on the human environment, is frequently the focus of attention.

Electromagnetic Fields Derived from Their Natural Sources

The magnetic field of the Earth is produced by the movement of molten iron in the outer core of the planet, which causes the Earth to generate its own magnetic field. This geomagnetic field is relatively steady, and it serves as a reference for navigation for a great number of animals. Localized deviations, which are referred to as geomagnetic anomalies, can take place, and they are occasionally linked to the occurrence of paranormal phenomena.

Constant bombardment of the Earth by cosmic rays, which are high-energy particles that originate from outer space, is referred to as cosmic radiation. Despite the fact that they are mostly composed of charged particles, electromagnetic radiation can be produced as a result of their contact with the atmosphere of the Earth. There is a possibility that certain regions that experience higher cosmic ray intensity will have enhanced electromagnetic activity.

Solar Activity: Solar flares and coronal mass ejections released by the Sun have the potential to exert an influence on the magnetosphere of the Earth, which can result in changes in geomagnetic activity. There is a hypothesis that suggests that greater paranormal encounters are associated with solar events, particularly during times of increasing solar activity.

Electromagnetic Fields Derived from Man-Made Contributions

Power Lines and Electrical Wiring: The transmission and distribution of electrical power both require substantial networks of power lines and wiring to accomplish their respective functions. Electromagnetic fields are produced by these systems, and the intensity of these fields is observed to be higher in close proximity to power lines. According to the findings of several studies, prolonged exposure to electromagnetic fields may have adverse consequences on one's health.

Electronic Devices: The electromagnetic landscape is influenced by the spread of electronic devices, which includes everything from computers and mobile phones to home appliances and other electronic gadgets. When compared to the frequencies that are related with paranormal events, the frequencies that are associated with these devices are often higher. However, concerns have been expressed concerning the potential health implications of these devices.

Radiofrequency and Microwave Radiation: Electronic devices and appliances that emit radiofrequency and microwave radiation include wireless fidelity (Wi-Fi), mobile phones, and microwave ovens. There are some paranormal investigations that suggest there may be relationships between the use of these fields and claimed hauntings, despite the fact that these fields operate at higher frequencies.

Electromagnetic Fields and the Experience of the Paranormal

The concept that oscillations in electromagnetic fields can be linked to encounters with the supernatural, such as hauntings, gained hold as a result of anecdotal tales and observations. According to a number of hypotheses, electromagnetic fields have the potential to exert an influence on persons and may contribute to the experience of paranormal activity.

Some experts have hypothesized that certain people may be more susceptible to changes in electromagnetic fields than others. This hypothesis is based on the human brain's sensitivity. Because the brain is an electrochemical organ, it is susceptible to being influenced by electromagnetic disturbances from the outside world. This could result in altered states of consciousness, vivid dreams, or hallucinations.

Theories of Residual Energy Paranormal investigators frequently investigate the concept of residual energy, which can be defined as energy imprints that are left behind by traumatic or intensely emotional life experiences. It has been hypothesized that these imprints might potentially influence the electromagnetic environment of a particular site, which would then result in the occurrence of paranormal occurrences.

Environmental Triggers, such as fluctuations in electromagnetic waves, have the potential to act as environmental triggers for paranormal experiences. The idea proposes that certain thresholds or patterns of electromagnetic activity may activate the human sensory system, which may result in the perception of apparitions, unusual sounds, or other occurrences that are considered to be on the other side of the psychic spectrum.

Investigations and studies conducted by scientists

Even though there are numerous anecdotal stories that show a connection between electromagnetic fields and paranormal encounters, the scientific community continues to exercise caution when it comes to establishing definitive findings. Studies that are conducted with the intention of establishing a causal connection between electromagnetic fields and hauntings confront a number of obstacles, including the following:

Due to the fact that paranormal encounters are often diverse and frequently unpredictable, there is a lack of consistency. A consistent association between variations in electromagnetic fields and claimed hauntings is difficult to establish due to the various nature of paranormal occurrences. This is because of the fact that electromagnetic fields fluctuate.

Methodological Problems: Many studies into the paranormal do not feature defined techniques and controls, which makes it difficult to reproduce the results of these investigations. The construction of a solid scientific foundation for the electromagnetic hypothesis is hampered by the lack of experiments that have been carefully prepared.

The role of psychological elements, such as suggestibility and belief in the paranormal, is not something that can be ignored. Both of these examples are examples of psychological factors. It is possible that people who visit places that are said to be haunted are more likely to perceive variations in electromagnetic fields as being of a supernatural nature, which can have an effect on their experiences.

The diversity of environmental elements, which includes differences in natural and man-made electromagnetic fields, presents difficulties in isolating specific influences on reported paranormal experiences. Some of these aspects include fluctuations in electromagnetic fields. The distinction between correlation and causality continues to be a question that has to be answered.

A dynamic junction of physics, psychology, and the investigation of the paranormal is represented by the investigation into the role that electromagnetic fields play in hauntings being investigated.

Despite the abundance of anecdotal evidence and speculations, the scientific community continues to take a cautious position, putting an emphasis on the necessity of conducting rigorous investigations and obtaining results that can be reproduced.

It is necessary to take a multidisciplinary approach because of the complexity of the paranormal terrain, as well as the difficulties associated with conducting controlled studies. Researchers continue to travel the unseen terrain in an effort to gain a better understanding of the potential connections that exist between electromagnetic fields and reported paranormal experiences. They are drawing on resources from the domains of physics, psychology, and parapsychology.

It is possible that the investigation of electromagnetic fields in the context of hauntings will produce findings that contribute to our greater knowledge of the intriguing interplay between the seen and the unseen as technology continues to progress and research approaches continue to evolve. The trip into the realms of the paranormal continues to captivate the curiosity of both scientists and enthusiasts alike. Whether electromagnetic fields act as triggers for altered states of consciousness or play a part in the persistence of residual energy imprints, the adventure into the realms of the paranormal continues to fascinate our curiosity.

| 48 |

Chapter 4

Technological Tools for Ethereal Exploration

One aspect of human curiosity that has persisted throughout history is the desire to investigate the ethereal and the supernatural. Despite the fact that traditional methods frequently involved mysticism, folklore, and spiritual practices, the incorporation of technology has opened up new frontiers in the exploration of the ethereal realm. Within the scope of this all-encompassing investigation, a wide variety of technological instruments that are utilized in the quest to comprehend the supernatural are investigated. These tools bridge the gap between the realms of science and the supernatural, offering fresh insights into long-standing mysteries. These tools range from advanced sensors and augmented reality to various devices that are used for ghost hunting.

Historical Perspectives on the Exploration of Ethereal Concepts

In order to have a proper understanding of the historical context of ethereal exploration, it is essential to have a prior understanding of contemporary technological tools. Techniques for communicating with or comprehending the supernatural have been developed by a variety of cultures throughout the course of history. For the purpose of gaining insights from the ethereal realm, various divination tools were utilized. These tools included pendulums, dowsing rods, and crystal balls.

Individuals who were thought to have a stronger connection to the spirit world were known as mediums, and they were an essential component in the process of conducting séances and communicating with those who had passed on. Despite the fact that these practices were steeped in mysticism and spirituality, they were instrumental in laying the groundwork for the intersection of technology and the supernatural in the modern era.

Ghost Hunting Equipment: Going Beyond the Veil

The practice of ghost hunting, which has its origins in the aspiration to communicate with and record paranormal entities, has undergone significant development as a result of the proliferation of technology. Contemporary ghost hunting expeditions make use of a wide variety of devices, each of which is designed to detect, measure, or communicate with the ethereal.

Electromagnetic Field (EMF) Meters: For those conducting investigations into the paranormal, EMF meters are among the most frequently used tools. They do this by measuring fluctuations in electromagnetic fields, operating under the assumption that ghosts or other entities may have an effect on these fields. EMF readings that contain spikes or patterns that are not typical are frequently interpreted as possible evidence of paranormal activity.

Thermal Imaging Cameras: Thermal imaging cameras are able to detect infrared radiation, which enables investigators to visualize temperature variations in their surroundings. The hypothesis proposes that entities could emerge as hot or cold spots in the environment. Thermal imaging is used to capture anomalies, which are then analyzed to determine whether or not they have any potential paranormal significance.

Digital Voice Recorders: Digital voice recorders are utilized in order to record electronic voice phenomena (EVP), which are voices or sounds that cannot be explained and are not audible during the investigation. For the purpose of identifying possible communication from the supernatural, investigators listen to recordings of recorded audio.

Electronic devices that rapidly scan through radio frequencies in order to generate a stream of white noise are referred to as ghost boxes or spirit boxes. Ghost boxes and spirit boxes are both types of electronic devices. There is a widespread belief that ghosts are able to manipulate this noise in order to produce audible responses or messages. The relevant responses are interpreted by paranormal investigators as possible communication from the other side.

Vibration Detectors and Motion Sensors: Motion sensors and vibration detectors are utilized for the purpose of indicating the presence of physical disturbances in the surrounding environment. There is a possibility that sudden movements or vibrations that cannot be attributed to any known causes could be perceived as evidence of paranormal activity.

Measurement of the Unseen Through the Use of Sensor Technologies

An expansion of the toolkit for ethereal exploration has been made possible by developments in sensor technologies. These advancements have provided investigators with sophisticated instruments that can measure and record paranormal phenomena. The use of these sensors, which are frequently utilized in scientific research, provides a more quantitative approach to investigations of the paranormal.

Various environmental factors, such as temperature, humidity, barometric pressure, and air quality, are measured by these sensors, which are used for environmental monitoring.

The changes that occur in these parameters are tracked in order to identify any correlations with the paranormal activity that has been reported.

Geiger Counters: Geiger counters are devices that detect ionizing radiation. Some paranormal investigators use these devices to identify potential radiation anomalies that are associated with supernatural occurrences. According to one theory, the presence of anomalous radiation is a sign that paranormal entities are out there manifesting themselves.

Some people believe that fluctuations in the magnetic field of the Earth are connected to paranormal activity. Geomagnetic sensors are used to monitor these fluctuations. In order to measure variations in the magnetic field, geomagnetic sensors are utilized. These sensors can provide investigators with data that can be analyzed to identify patterns or correlations.

Instruments that detect infrasound Infrasound, which consists of sound waves that are below the threshold of human hearing, have been linked to feelings of unease and even experiences that are considered to be paranormal. The use of infrasound detectors allows for the identification of low-frequency vibrations that may coincide with ethereal phenomena or phenomena that have been reported.

Virtual and Augmented Reality: Bridging the Gap Between Actualities

The combination of technologies known as augmented reality (AR) and virtual reality (VR) has brought about a revolutionary change in the manner in which individuals interact with various supernatural phenomena. Users are able to interact with simulated environments or superimpose digital information on the real world through the use of these immersive technologies, which offer new opportunities for ethereal exploration.

Augmented Reality Ghost Hunting Augmented reality ghost hunting applications make use of the cameras and sensors found on smartphones to superimpose virtual elements on the real world. At the same time that the app superimposes ghostly apparitions, paranormal hotspots, or historical information related to reported supernatural occurrences, users are able to explore their surroundings.

Virtual Reality Simulations: Virtual reality simulations are designed to transport users to immersive digital environments that are designed to replicate haunted locations or paranormal scenarios. By using virtual reality (VR), investigators are able to recreate historical events, which enables them to gain a more in-depth understanding of the circumstances surrounding alleged supernatural activities.

Reconstructions in Digital Form: Augmented reality (AR) and virtual reality (VR) technologies make it possible to create digital reconstructions of haunted locations or scenes associated with extraordinary occurrences. Investigators have the ability to investigate these reconstructions, examine the details, and possibly discover new insights into the ethereal phenomena that have been brought to light.

The Uncovering of Patterns Through the Use of Artificial Intelligence and Data Analysis

Artificial intelligence (AI) is playing an increasingly important role in the process of discovering patterns, correlations, and anomalies. This is because the abundance of data that is collected during ethereal exploration necessitates the use of sophisticated analysis tools. Artificial intelligence applications improve the effectiveness and objectivity of data analysis in investigations involving the paranormal.

Pattern Recognition Algorithms: Pattern recognition algorithms powered by artificial intelligence analyze large datasets in order to identify recurring patterns or correlations that may not be obvious to human investigators. Trends that are associated with reported paranormal activity can be uncovered with the help of this.

Analysis of Speech and Sentiment Artificial intelligence tools for speech and sentiment analysis are utilized in the process of evaluating recorded audio, particularly in the context of online video conferences (EVP). These technologies have the ability to recognize patterns of speech, emotional content, and possibly even reveal messages or responses from the supernatural that have been concealed.

Automated Environmental Monitoring: Artificial intelligence has the ability to automate the analysis of data collected by environmental sensors, thereby identifying patterns or irregularities that may coincide with reported instances of paranormal activity. This not only makes the investigation process more efficient but also makes it easier for investigators to receive alerts in real time.

In the context of technological ethereal exploration, ethical considerations are present

It is becoming increasingly important to take ethical considerations into account when conducting ethereal exploration as technology continues to advance. It is essential to strike a balance between scientific rigor and respect for individuals, individual beliefs, and cultural contexts in order to guarantee responsible and ethical practices in the field of paranormal investigations.

Consent to Participate: It is of the utmost importance to obtain informed consent from individuals who are participating in ethereal exploration experiments. The purpose of the investigation, the manner in which technology will be utilized, and any potential psychological or emotional impact on participants must be communicated in a clear and concise manner by the investigators.

Ethereal exploration frequently intersects with cultural practices and beliefs, so it is important to be sensitive to these intersections. Those conducting investigations are required to approach communities and locations with cultural sensitivity, showing respect for the local customs and traditions that are associated with the supernatural.

Concerns Regarding Privacy The utilization of technology, particularly in the context of augmented or virtual reality experiences, gives rise to concerns regarding privacy. It is imperative that investigators take into consideration the impact that their actions may have on individuals who may be captured in photographs, videos, or digital reconstructions. This will ensure that the rights to privacy are protected.

Transparency in the Use of Technology It is critical to maintain transparency with regard to the utilization of technology. It is important for investigators to communicate the capabilities and limitations of the tools they use in a clear and concise manner. This will help to cultivate trust and understanding among participants as well as the general public.

Scientific investigation and the search for an understanding of the supernatural have come together in a fascinating way through the development of technological tools for ethereal exploration. The use of these tools opens up new avenues for the investigation of paranormal phenomena. These tools include advanced sensors, ghost hunting devices, augmented reality, and artificial intelligence. Nevertheless, as technological advancements continue, ethical considerations need to be taken into account in order to ensure that these tools are used in a responsible manner when exploring the ethereum.

Traditional boundaries are being challenged by the interaction between science and the supernatural, which calls for an approach that draws from a variety of fields, including physics, psychology, cultural studies, and technology. Investigators navigate a complex terrain that requires both technical expertise and ethical mindfulness. Whether they are looking to capture evidence of paranormal entities, recreate historical scenes, or analyze environmental data, they are navigating a terrain that is complex.

The interface between science and the supernatural continues to be a frontier that is ready to be explored, despite the fact that our understanding of technology and the ethereal world is evolving. With the combination of a commitment to ethical practices and the incorporation of emerging technologies, there is the possibility of gaining new insights into the mysteries that have captivated the human imagination for centuries. As the journey into the unknown continues, the curiosity to uncover the mysteries of the supernatural realm is the driving force behind the undertaking.

4.1 Ghost-Hunting Equipment: From EMF meters to infrared cameras

Throughout the years, there has been a significant evolution in the pursuit of paranormal phenomena. Ghost hunters now use a wide variety of specialized equipment in order to identify, quantify, and record supernatural occurrences. Whether it be the traditional use of electromagnetic field (EMF) meters or the more advanced use of infrared cameras and audio recording devices, these tools are extremely important in the process of deciphering the mysteries of the paranormal. The purpose of this investigation is to investigate the various types of ghost-hunting equipment, focusing on their functions, applications, and contributions to the investigation of haunted locations.

Indicators of Electromagnetic Field (EMF): Identifying Energies That Are Not Visible

Introducing Electromagnetic Field (EMF) Meters Electromagnetic field (EMF) meters are essential instruments in the field of paranormal investigations. Variations in electromagnetic fields are measured by these devices, which operate under the presumption that paranormal entities may have the ability to influence or disrupt these fields. A sensor that detects changes in electromagnetic radiation and a display that provides a visual or audible indication of fluctuations are the two components that are typically included in electromagnetic field meters (EMF meters).

Speculations Regarding Electromagnetic Field Readings Ghost hunters frequently make the connection between spikes in EMF readings and the presence of paranormal activity. As part of their manifestation, ghosts or spirits may be able to generate or manipulate electromagnetic fields, according to the theory that is currently in the prevalent position. As a consequence of this, investigators make use of electromagnetic field meters in order to locate areas that exhibit unusual electromagnetic activity.

Applications in Paranormal Investigations Electromagnetic field meters are frequently utilized in the course of ghost hunts and investigations that take place at locations that are rumored to be haunted. While moving through the environment, investigators take note of any changes in electromagnetic fields and document any correlations that may exist with the experiences that have been reported as being paranormal.

Readings of electromagnetic fields (EMF) are frequently recorded alongside other data, which contributes to an all-encompassing investigation of the haunted location.

When it comes to visualizing temperature anomalies, infrared cameras and thermal imaging

The use of infrared cameras in ghost hunting Infrared (IR) cameras and thermal imaging devices are extremely important in the field of ghost hunting because they are able to capture images that reach beyond the visible light spectrum. Because these devices are able to detect heat signatures and variations in temperature, they have the potential to reveal anomalies that are associated with supernatural entities. Night-vision capabilities are frequently included in infrared cameras, which enables investigators to explore dark environments with improved visibility.

When it comes to the visualization of cold and hot spots, paranormal investigators have a theory that ghosts may appear in the form of cold or hot spots in the environment. The use of infrared cameras makes it possible to visualize these temperature variations, which in turn enables the identification of anomalous areas that may be sites of concentrated paranormal activity. The presence of spirits is frequently mentioned in connection with cold spots, whereas the presence of energy manifestations may be indicated by hot spots.

Applications in the field of paranormal photography Infrared photography involves more than just video recording; it also involves taking still photographs. In order to capture photographs in low-light conditions, ghost hunters use cameras that are equipped with infrared technology. These photographs help reveal potential apparitions, energy patterns, or other unexplained phenomena. In investigations into the paranormal, the examination of these photographs adds to the body of evidence that is being gathered.

Digital voice recorders, which are used to record electronic voice phenomena (EVP)

The significance of Electronic Voice Phenomena (EVP) Electronic Voice Phenomena (EVP) refers to sounds or voices that cannot be explained and are captured on audio recordings, typically during investigations into the paranormal. There is a widespread belief among ghost hunters that these enigmatic voices could be a form of communication from the spirit world. In order to record and document instances of electronic voice phenomena (EVP), digital voice recorders are indispensable tools.

EVP sessions are conducted by paranormal investigators, during which they ask questions or encourage potential entities to communicate. An analysis of the recordings is performed after the sessions have been recorded. In order to collect audio data, digital voice recorders are strategically placed in haunted locations using surveillance technology.

Following the conclusion of the investigation, analysts examine recordings, identifying and making improvements to potential EVP instances for further investigation.

In addition to basic playback, investigators use advanced audio analysis software to filter, amplify, and analyze recorded sounds. This software is used in addition to basic playback. It is possible that this software will assist in the identification of subtle voices, whispers, or anomalies that may not be immediately noticeable. From the audio that has been recorded, the objective is to extract responses or messages that can be understood.

The Real-Time Communication Tools That Are Ghost Boxes and Spirit Boxes
A Brief Explanation of Ghost Boxes Ghost boxes, which are also referred to as spirit boxes, are electronic devices that are designed to rapidly scan through radio frequencies. It is believed that these devices, which provide a continuous stream of audio snippets, make it possible to communicate with spirits in real time. Those who are interested in ghost hunting interpret the responses they receive through the device as possible messages from the supernatural realm.

Principles of Operation Ghost boxes are typically designed to sweep through AM or FM radio frequencies at a high speed, thereby producing a continuous flow of white noise within the environment. Spirits are thought to be able to manipulate this noise in order to form coherent responses or messages, according to the theory. When responses that are coherent and relevant are perceived, the randomness of radio snippets is considered to be significant.

Applications in Paranormal Communication Ghost boxes are used during investigations as a form of interactive communication with potential spirits. This practice is known as "paranormal communication." Those conducting the investigation will ask questions, and if they receive responses, they will be regarded as direct communication from the opposing party. Due to the fact that ghost boxes operate in real time, they bring an element of immediacy to investigations into the paranormal.

It is possible to detect physical manifestations through the use of motion sensors and vibration detectors
Motion sensors and vibration detectors are instruments that are utilized in the process of identifying physical disturbances or movements in the environment. Motion sensors are utilized in the field of paranormal investigations. These devices are utilized

by investigators of the paranormal in order to identify unexplained shifts or activity that may coincide with reported paranormal occurrences. Strange movements may be an indication of the presence of a ghost or other supernatural being.

Technologies for Detecting Vibration Vibration detectors are devices that monitor and record variations in the intensity of vibrations that occur in the surrounding area. Vibrations that are brought on suddenly or unexpectedly and cannot be attributed to any known sources may give rise to suspicions of paranormal activity. For the purpose of gaining a comprehensive understanding of the environment in which the investigation is taking place, these detectors are frequently used in conjunction with other tools.

Applications in Triggering Equipment Motion sensors and vibration detectors are sometimes incorporated into ghost-hunting setups in order to trigger other equipment, such as cameras or audio recorders, in response to activity that has been detected. With the help of this automation, investigators are able to record potentially significant moments without the need for significant human intervention.

The Geiger Counter: Investigating Radiation Anomalies in the World

Geiger Counters: An Introduction Geiger counters are instruments that are designed to detect ionizing radiation. In the field of ghost hunting, geiger counters are utilized by paranormal investigators to identify potential radiation anomalies associated with paranormal phenomena. Geiger counters are primarily utilized in scientific contexts. According to one theory, the presence of anomalous radiation is a sign that paranormal entities are out there manifesting themselves.

Theories Regarding Radiation and Other Forms of Extraterrestrial Acts:

There is a suggested connection between increased levels of ionizing radiation and the appearance of spirits or entities, according to certain theories that are associated with the paranormal. Geiger counters are utilized during paranormal investigations, particularly in locations that have been reported to have ghostly encounters. The reasons for this proposed connection are still the subject of speculation; however, geiger counters are used to measure radiation levels.

Applications in Haunted Environments Geiger counters are utilized by paranormal investigators in order to investigate locations that have been reported to be having ghostly activity. The purpose of this endeavor is to identify patterns of radiation that may coincide with paranormal phenomena that have been reported. Geiger counters that are incorporated into the investigation add a scientific dimension to the investigation by allowing for the examination of environmental factors that may be responsible for ethereal occurrences.

The equipment used in ghost hunting, which includes electromagnetic field (EMF) meters, infrared cameras, and ghost boxes, is a representative example of the combination of scientific instruments and the pursuit of understanding the mysteries of the supernatural.

These devices, which are utilized by investigators in haunted locations all over the world, contribute to the documentation and analysis of supernatural phenomena that have been reported. The use of specialized tools brings a level of precision and objectivity to the investigation of the ethereal, despite the fact that debates continue to take place regarding the scientific validity of investigations into the paranormal.

As technological advancements continue, it is likely that new tools and methodologies will emerge, which will provide new perspectives on mysteries that have been around for centuries. The dynamic interplay between science and the supernatural, which is made possible by ghost-hunting equipment, exemplifies the ongoing fascination that humans have with the unknown. When it comes to capturing unexplained sounds, visualizing temperature anomalies, or attempting to communicate with the spirit world in real time, investigators navigate a realm in which the lines between what can be seen and what cannot be seen become increasingly blurry.

Ghost hunters are at the intersection of scientific inquiry and the age-old human curiosity about the afterlife. They engage in the pursuit of understanding the paranormal in order to gain deeper insights into the supernatural. The exploration of haunted locations continues to captivate the imagination, offering glimpses into the mysterious realm that lies beyond our everyday perception. This is because technology is constantly evolving, and our understanding of the ethereum is growing deeper.

4.2 Advancements in Paranormal Research: The intersection of tech and the supernatural

The investigation of the supernatural has undergone a transformational journey, particularly with the incorporation of cutting-edge technology into the conventional methods of investigation. A fascinating intersection where scientific tools, data analytics, and emerging technologies meet the mysteries of the supernatural is represented by the advancements that have been made in the field of paranormal research. This investigation delves into the development of research on the paranormal, the part that technology plays in determining the structure of investigations, and the influence that these technological advancements have had on our comprehension of the unexplained.

The Development of Research Concerning the Paranormal

The human race has been fascinated by supernatural occurrences for centuries, which has resulted in the development of a wide range of cultural, spiritual, and religious practices that are aimed at gaining an understanding of the supernatural. Mysticism, folklore, and divination were frequently utilized in the early approaches in order to connect with or interpret the unseen occurrences.

The beginnings of scientific inquiry can be traced back to the 19th and 20th centuries, when there was a shift toward the use of scientific methodologies in the investigation of paranormal phenomena. The Society for Psychical Research (SPR), which was established in 1882, was one of the organizations that endeavored to apply scientific principles to the investigation of paranormal phenomena. This marked the beginning of an approach to the supernatural that was more systematic and had a stronger foundation in evidence.

Challenges and Skepticism: Despite the development of scientific frameworks, research on the paranormal was met with skepticism from the scientific communities that are prevalent in mainstream science. The fact that paranormal experiences are considered to be subjective, in addition to the absence of evidence that can be replicated, contributed to the difficulties that researchers encountered when attempting to gain wider acceptance.

The Importance of Technology in the Investigation of Paranormal Occurrences

An Introduction to the Role of Technology in Paranormal Research The incorporation of technology into paranormal investigations has completely reshaped the landscape of research. Researchers are now able to collect, analyze, and document data with a level of precision and objectivity that was previously unattainable thanks to the innovations brought about by modern tools.

The term "ghost-hunting equipment" has become synonymous with the term "paranormal investigations." This equipment includes electromagnetic field (EMF) meters, infrared cameras, and audio recording devices, along with other similar devices. Investigators are able to examine the recordings and measurements that these tools provide in order to look for anomalies that are associated with the paranormal activity that has been reported.

Developments in Sensor Technologies: The range of measurable data in the field of paranormal research has expanded as a result of developments in sensor technologies. Environmental monitoring sensors, geomagnetic sensors, and infrasound detectors all contribute to a more comprehensive understanding of the conditions that are associated with hauntings that have been reported.

Augmented and Virtual Reality: The utilization of technologies that utilize augmented reality (AR) and virtual reality (VR) has introduced a new facet to the investigation of paranormal phenomena. Researchers have the ability to recreate haunted environments, superimpose digital information on physical surroundings, and even simulate historical events, all of which contribute to a more immersive experience when investigating the supernatural.

Artificial Intelligence and Data Analysis: Methods of advanced data analysis are required because of the large amount of data that is generated during investigations into paranormal phenomena. Researchers are able to uncover patterns, correlations, and anomalies within the data that they have collected with the assistance of applications that utilize artificial intelligence (AI). These applications include pattern recognition algorithms and speech analysis tools.

Recent Developments in the Equipment Used for Ghost Hunting

EMF Meters: Going Beyond Fluctuations: EMF meters, which were once restricted to detecting fluctuations in electromagnetic fields, have progressed to include features such as data logging and real-time monitoring. Because of this, investigators are able to monitor and analyze changes in electromagnetic activity over extended periods of time, which provides a more nuanced understanding of the influences of the environment.

Technologies such as infrared cameras and thermal imaging can improve visuals

Both the resolution and sensitivity of infrared cameras and thermal imaging devices have made significant strides in recent years. With the help of high-definition visuals, investigators are able to capture and analyze temperature variations with greater precision, which has the potential to reveal more subtle anomalies associated with reported paranormal phenomena.

Digital Voice Recorders: Advanced Audio Analysis These days, digital voice recorders come pre-loaded with features that allow for advanced audio analysis. These features, which include built-in filters, noise reduction capabilities, and speech-to-text functionalities, make it possible for investigators to conduct more in-depth examinations of recorded audio in search of possible instances of electronic voice recognition (EVP).

Interaction in Real Time with Ghost Boxes and Spirit Boxes: Virtual Reality

Several technological advancements have been made to ghost boxes and spirit boxes. These advancements include the incorporation of noise reduction filters, adjustable scanning speeds, and user-friendly interfaces in some of the devices. The purpose of these enhancements is to make it easier to interact and communicate with potential spirits in real time while investigations are being conducted.

An Intelligent Automation System Comprised of Motion Sensors and Vibration Detectors

In recent years, motion sensors and vibration detectors have undergone significant advancements, incorporating capabilities for intelligent automation. There are some devices that are able to differentiate between normal environmental movements and what could be considered paranormal activity. This helps to reduce the number of false positives and improves the reliability of events that are triggered.

Techniques and Applications of Technology in the Study of the Paranormal

Remote Investigations: The advancement of technology has made it possible for researchers to conduct remote investigations, which involves exploring haunted locations without physically being present. The ability to investigate and document paranormal phenomena from a distance is made possible by technologies such as live-streaming cameras, remote-controlled devices, and virtual reality simulations.

Data Sharing and Collaboration: The advent of the digital age has made it easier for researchers working on paranormal phenomena all over the world to share and collaborate on data. Investigators are able to share their findings, discuss methodologies, and collectively analyze patterns all through the use of online platforms, databases, and forums. This helps to foster a collaborative and global approach to the investigation of paranormal phenomena.

Engagement of the Public and Education of Enthusiasts Technology has been an essential component in the process of educating enthusiasts about paranormal research and captivating the public's attention. The use of social media, podcasts, and online platforms gives researchers the opportunity to disseminate their findings, present evidence, and engage with a more extensive network of people. As a result, this helps to cultivate a sense of community and encourages open conversation about the supernatural.

Ethical Considerations and Obstacles to Overcome

When it comes to privacy and consent, the use of technology in paranormal research raises ethical concerns that need to be taken into consideration. Whether they are participating in the investigation in person or remotely, researchers have a responsibility to ensure that individuals who are participating in the investigation are fully informed about the use of recording equipment and the potential public dissemination of findings.

A sensitivity to culture is required because investigations into the paranormal frequently intersect with cultural practices and beliefs. Researchers have a responsibility to approach haunted communities and locations with cultural sensitivity, acknowledging and honoring the local customs and traditions that are associated with the supernatural.

Skepticism and Scientific Rigor: The incorporation of technology does not eliminate the skepticism that surrounds research on the paranormal. In order for researchers to achieve wider acceptance, they need to adhere to the standards of scientific rigor, carry out controlled experiments, and ensure that their methodologies are transparent.

An exciting new era has begun, one in which the supernatural and scientific inquiry are coming together. This era is marked by advancements in paranormal research, which are driven by the integration of technology. Through the use of technology, ghost hunters and researchers are able to navigate this intersection with a precision that goes beyond the methods that have been traditionally used, thereby opening up new avenues for exploration and comprehension.

The lines between what can be seen and what cannot be seen are becoming increasingly blurry as technology continues to advance, providing researchers with tools that have never been seen before to help them solve the mysteries of the paranormal. Whether it be through the use of enhanced infrared cameras to capture spectral anomalies, through the use of advanced ghost boxes to engage in real-time communication, or through the use of artificial intelligence to analyze vast datasets, the modern paranormal investigator is at the forefront of a field that is both dynamic and multidisciplinary.

Not only does the journey into the supernatural, which is guided by technology, invite seasoned researchers, but it also invites a curious public that is eager to explore the elements that cannot be explained. Embracing the mystery of the unseen with a spirit of curiosity and scientific inquiry, the intersection of technology and the supernatural encourages us to question, investigate, and embrace things that are beyond our ability to see. As we make our way through this ever-changing landscape, the pursuit of the paranormal promises to continue to be an intriguing exploration of the mysterious realms that lie beyond our everyday comprehension.

4.3 The Ethics of Ghost Hunting: Balancing curiosity with respect for the unknown

The pursuit of paranormal phenomena and encounters with the supernatural, also known as ghost hunting, has become increasingly popular in recent years. This trend can be attributed to people's natural curiosity and fascination with the unknown. It is essential to take into consideration the ethical implications that are associated with this field, despite the fact that the pursuit of evidence of ghosts and spirits is motivated by a genuine desire to investigate the mysteries of the afterlife. During this investigation, the ethical considerations of ghost hunting are investigated, and the delicate balance that must be maintained between satiating curiosity and showing respect for the unknown is investigated.

The Participant's Well-Being and the Informed Consent Process

Respect for the Living: When it comes to ghost hunting, one of the most important ethical considerations revolves around the people who are involved, whether they are investigators, clients, or participants in paranormal experiments. It is of the utmost importance to respect the well-being and gain the consent of all parties involved.

Before conducting investigations in private residences or public spaces, ghost hunters are required to obtain informed consent from the owners of the property, residents of the area, and any other individuals who may be affected by the exploration.

In order to gather possible evidence of paranormal activity, ghost hunters frequently make use of a wide variety of tools, including audio and video recording devices. This raises concerns about privacy. Keeping in mind the concerns regarding privacy and making certain that the rights and personal boundaries of the individuals who are being recorded are respected is of the utmost importance. The use of private information or photographs without the owner's permission may constitute a violation of both ethical and privacy standards.

Ghost hunting can be an emotionally charged experience, particularly for individuals who have had personal encounters with the supernatural or who reside in allegedly haunted locations. However, there are ways to minimize the emotional distress that can be experienced during this activity. Ethical ghost hunters place a high priority on reducing the participants' sense of emotional distress and the psychological impact they experience. Providing clear information about the investigation process, potential outcomes, and the possibility of encountering unsettling phenomena is a necessary step in this process.

Sensitivity to different cultures and respect for different beliefs

Paranormal encounters frequently intersect with cultural and religious beliefs, which adds an additional layer of complexity to investigations. These encounters can be difficult to navigate. Individuals who are interested in ghost hunting are required to approach haunted locations with cultural sensitivity, taking into account the variety of spiritual and religious perspectives. Respecting the local customs, traditions, and belief systems that are associated with the supernatural is considered to be of the utmost importance.

Avoiding Exploitation It is imperative that the investigation of haunted locations steer clear of sensationalism and the exploitation of cultural or religious symbols. When paranormal experiences are sensationalized for the purpose of entertainment, it can be disrespectful to the beliefs of the communities and individuals involved. When it comes to ghost hunting, ethical practices put an emphasis on understanding and learning from a variety of perspectives rather than sensationalizing the supernatural.

Collaboration with Spiritual Leaders Ghost hunters may take into consideration the possibility of collaborating with local spiritual leaders or authorities in situations where their investigations intersect with particular religious or spiritual practices. The use of this collaborative approach not only helps to promote understanding, but it also guarantees that the investigation will be carried out in a manner that is in line with the beliefs and values held by the community.

The Responsible Application of Technology

Ensuring that Privacy Rights Are Respected The use of technology, such as audio and video recording devices, infrared cameras, and motion sensors, raises ethical concerns that are related to privacy rights. Before conducting recordings in private or public areas, ghost hunters are required to obtain consent and be transparent about the technology they use. One of the most important aspects of responsible ghost hunting is treating individuals and property owners with respect for their privacy.

Some ghost-hunting tools, such as ghost boxes or spirit boxes, are designed to interpret random electronic signals as potential communication from spirits. It is important to avoid misrepresenting technology in this way. They should avoid misrepresenting the capabilities of such devices and communicate openly about the speculative nature of their interpretations. Ethical ghost hunters should avoid lying about the capabilities of such devices. When it comes to presenting evidence and findings, honesty is absolutely necessary in order to keep one's integrity in the field.

In order to guarantee the safety of their data, ghost hunters frequently disseminate their discoveries and evidence to a wider audience. This is made possible by the proliferation of digital platforms and online communities. In order to protect sensitive information and ensure the safety of data, it is absolutely necessary to take precautions. When conducting investigations, ethical ghost hunters take precautions to protect the privacy of individuals who are involved in the investigation and to prevent the unauthorized use of content that has been recorded.

Rigor and skepticism in the scientific community

Maintaining Scientific Standards The field of paranormal research is frequently met with skepticism from the scientific community due to the subjective nature of ghost encounters and the lack of evidence that can be reproduced at the same time. Ghost hunters who are committed to ethics make it a priority to conduct their investigations in accordance with scientific standards. They employ stringent methodologies, controls, and documentation in order to bolster the credibility of their work.

In order to avoid exploiting paranormal phenomena for the purpose of entertainment, ethical ghost hunters resist the temptation to exploit these phenomena for the purpose of entertainment, which would compromise the integrity of scientific research. On the other hand, responsible investigators place a higher priority on genuine exploration and the pursuit of knowledge than they do on the entertainment value of ghost hunting, despite the fact that television shows and the media may sensationalize ghost hunting for dramatic effect.

Acceptance of Skepticism: An ethical approach to ghost hunting requires accepting skepticism and engaging in critical inquiry throughout the process. It is important for ghost hunters to be open to alternative explanations for the phenomena that they have reported, as they should recognize that not every unexplained occurrence may be that of the supernatural. It is important to be transparent about the limitations of investigations and the uncertainties that exist in order to contribute to a responsible and balanced approach.

A foundation that is built on ethics and respect is necessary for ghost hunting, which is driven by a human curiosity about the mysteries of the afterlife. For the purpose of preserving the credibility of paranormal research, it is essential to strike a balance between this curiosity and a mindful approach to informed consent, cultural sensitivity, responsible technology use, and scientific rigor.

Not only do ethical ghost hunters endeavor to solve the mysteries of the supernatural, but they also make it a point to do so in a way that shows respect for the living, acknowledges the diversity of cultures, protects individuals' right to privacy, and operates in accordance with scientific principles. The ethical considerations that are outlined in this article serve as a compass for those who are navigating the complex terrain that lies between the visible and the invisible dimensions of the field as it continues to develop. It is possible to ensure that the pursuit of the unknown is carried out with integrity, compassion, and respect for the mysteries that captivate the human imagination by cultivating curiosity with ethical foundations.

Chapter 5

The Psychology of Ghostly Encounters

For a very long time, the realm of ghostly encounters has been able to captivate the human imagination, which has resulted in the creation of tales about spectral apparitions and phenomena that cannot be explained. The field of psychology provides fascinating insights into the complexities of perception, cognition, and the human mind, despite the fact that paranormal experiences are frequently attributed to the supernatural. The purpose of this in-depth investigation is to investigate the psychological aspects of ghostly encounters, specifically the cognitive and psychological factors that play a role in the perception of the supernatural.

The perception of the supernatural and the illusion of its existence

Sensory Perception and Ambiguity: It is common for ghostly encounters to start with non-specific sensory stimuli. When exposed to environments that are unfamiliar or have low levels of illumination, the brain may have difficulty accurately interpreting sensory information, which can result in erroneous perceptions of shadows, reflections, or everyday objects. One of the factors that can contribute to the formation of ghostly apparitions is the human tendency to fill in gaps in perception with patterns that are already seen.

Pattern Recognition and Pareidolia: The phenomenon of pareidolia, which is the tendency to recognize meaningful patterns or images in random stimuli, is an important factor in the occurrence of mysterious encounters. The perception of a ghostly presence can be triggered by a variety of sensory stimuli, including faces in shadows, figures in textured surfaces, or even familiar shapes in random noise. A factor that contributes to the formation of illusory apparitions is the tendency of the brain to impose order on stimuli that are normally chaotic.

Cognitive Biases: The interpretation of experiences can be influenced by cognitive biases, such as the confirmation bias and the expectancy bias. It is possible that people who have a strong belief in the supernatural are more likely to interpret ambiguous stimuli as manifestations of ghosts, which serves to reinforce the beliefs that they already hold. It is possible for the perception of paranormal phenomena to be influenced by the power of suggestion as well as a predisposition to seek confirmation.

Beliefs and cultural conditioning

The influence of belief systems on the formation of ghostly encounters is significant. Expectations also play a significant role in this regard. There is a correlation between individuals who have strong beliefs in the supernatural and the likelihood that they will interpret ambiguous stimuli as being abnormal. A significant factor that contributes to the subjective nature of ghostly experiences is the presence of expectations. These expectations can be influenced by cultural conditioning, religious beliefs, or exposure to media portrayals of ghosts.

Different cultures have different beliefs about the supernatural. The nature of ghostly encounters and how they are interpreted are significantly influenced by cultural factors. There are a variety of beliefs that people from various cultures hold regarding the supernatural, the afterlife, and spirits. The lens through which individuals perceive and interpret paranormal phenomena is shaped by the cultural differences that exist in folklore, traditions, and religious practices based on the individual.

The potency of suggestion Both social influence and the power of suggestion have the potential to play a significant part in the occurrence of ghostly encounters. Individuals may be more susceptible to suggestion when they are in a group setting or when they are conducting paranormal investigations. This can result in individuals having similar perceptions of ghostly activity. Group dynamics and a shared belief in the supernatural have the potential to amplify the intensity of reported encounters as well as the frequency with which they occur.

Psychological Considerations Regarding the Occurrence of Hauntings

Night Terrors and Sleep Paralysis Both sleep paralysis and night terrors provide psychological explanations for experiences that are frequently associated with hauntings. There is a possibility that individuals will experience a presence, feel pressure on their chest, and see shadowy figures when they are experiencing sleep paralysis. One of the factors that contributes to reports of ghostly encounters during the night is the presence of night terrors, which can involve intense feelings of fear as well as hallucinatory experiences.

Environmental factors, such as exposure to infrasound, electromagnetic fields, or environmental toxins, have the potential to induce hallucinations and other unusual perceptual experiences. Hallucinations can also be induced by environmental factors. There is a possibility that the presence of these elements is a contributing factor to reports of ghostly activity in haunted locations. In order to differentiate between genuine paranormal encounters and perceptual anomalies, it is essential to have a solid understanding of the impact that environmental influences have.

The relationship between psychological trauma and coping mechanisms suggests that people who have been through psychological trauma may be more likely to report ghostly encounters as a means of coping with their experiences. It is possible for the mind to attempt to process and make sense of traumatic experiences by presenting them in symbolic or metaphorical representations, which can result in the perception of spectral apparitions or haunting phenomena.

Disturbances in the Perception and Recollection of Time

Anomalies in time perception, such as time dilation, have been linked to paranormal experiences. Temporal lobe epilepsy is another condition that has been suggested to be associated with time dilation. Alterations in states of consciousness, hallucinations, and distorted perceptions of time are all symptoms that can be brought on by temporal lobe epilepsy, which is a condition that affects the temporal lobe of the brain. There is a possibility that people who suffer from this condition will report having experiences with apparitions or otherworldly entities.

Erroneous Attributions and Memory Distortions Both memory distortions and incorrect attributions play a role in the formation of ghostly encounters. There is a possibility of errors occurring in the testimony of witnesses, and memories can be influenced by factors such as suggestion, cultural narratives, or the desire to find a supernatural explanation. Due to the fact that memory is a reconstructive process, it can be difficult to differentiate between experiences that are genuine and those that are influenced by cognitive processes.

The Psychological Effects of Having Encounters with Ghosts

Paranormal Experiences and Post-Traumatic Stress Disorder (PTSD): What Are the Differences?

People may experience psychological repercussions as a result of ghostly encounters, particularly those that involve intense fear or a perceived potential threat. It is possible for people who have been through traumatic experiences to develop symptoms that are commonly associated with post-traumatic stress disorder (PTSD). When it comes to providing appropriate support and intervention, it is essential to have a profound understanding of the psychological impact that paranormal experiences have.

Mechanisms of Coping and Resilience: Some people find that believing in the paranormal and attributing their experiences to ghostly encounters are effective coping mechanisms. Resilience is another factor that can be considered. There is a possibility that the symbolic nature of ghosts can serve as a framework for the processing of challenging feelings or experiences.

Obtaining valuable insights into the human psyche can be accomplished through the investigation of coping strategies and resilience approaches within the context of paranormal beliefs.

An Examination of the Relationship Between Beliefs in the Paranormal and Mental Health

Relationship Between Beliefs in the Paranormal and Mental Health The connection between paranormal beliefs and mental health is a complicated one. While there are some people who find solace and meaning in supernatural explanations, there are also people who may experience distress or anxiety as a result of their beliefs. It is possible to gain insight into therapeutic approaches and provide individuals with support as they navigate their experiences by gaining an understanding of how paranormal beliefs intersect with mental health.

Perspectives on Counseling Regarding Encounters with the Paranormal:

A client-centered and culturally sensitive approach is taken by mental health professionals when they interact with individuals who report having ghostly encounters that they have experienced. Therapists are able to investigate the psychological impact of experiences, identify strategies for coping, and provide support that is tailored to the individual's specific requirements when they acknowledge the significance of paranormal beliefs within the individual's worldview.

When it comes to the intricate relationship that exists between perception, belief systems, and the human mind, the psychology of ghostly encounters provides a nuanced understanding of the human mind. Recognizing the psychological factors that are at play provides a more comprehensive understanding of ghostly phenomena, despite the fact that the supernatural may continue to continue to captivate and inspire awe.

As we make our way through the shadows of the mind, it becomes clear that ghostly encounters are formed by a wide variety of psychological processes. These processes include sensory perception, cultural influences, memory distortions, and coping mechanisms. This investigation encourages us to approach the supernatural with an attitude of curiosity, recognizing the diverse range of human experiences that contribute to the enduring allure of the realm of the ghosts. This allows us to gain a deeper understanding of the mysteries that lie within the mind, which is a place where the lines between reality and perception become increasingly blurry, and where the mystery of the supernatural continues to captivate the human spirit.

5.1 The Power of Belief: How expectation influences perception

One of the most fascinating aspects of human cognition is the complex relationship that exists between perception and belief. Individuals' interpretations of the world around them and their interactions with it are shaped by the power of belief, which in turn influences their experiences and in turn shapes their reality. For the purpose of this investigation, the profound influence that belief has on perception is investigated. Specifically, the ways in which expectations, which are influenced by cultural, social, and personal factors, can shape and even create our subjective reality are investigated.

The Elements Serving as the Basis for Belief and Perception

Cognitive Frameworks: Belief functions as a cognitive framework that individuals use to interpret the vast amount of sensory information that they come into contact with on a daily basis. The way in which individuals perceive, process, and make sense of their surroundings is influenced by this framework, which is developed through personal experiences, cultural influences, and social conditioning.

The role of expectation as a cognitive filter to shape perception Expectation serves as a cognitive filter that guides perception. When people have certain beliefs or expectations, their minds become attuned to information that aligns with those expectations, while at the same time they filter out or downplay information that contradicts those expectations. This selective attention has an effect on the construction of the individual's own particular reality.

The interpretation of sensory input by the brain is not a passive process; rather, it is actively shaped by beliefs and expectations. This is referred to as sensory perception and interpretation. Various sensory stimuli, including those that are visual, auditory, tactile, and others, are processed by an individual's cognitive framework, which ultimately results in the individual's subjective experience of reality.

The impact of cultural factors on beliefs and perceptions

Cultural Constructs and Worldviews: The influence of culture is a significant factor in the formation of belief systems and, as a result, perceptions. There is a correlation between the development of shared worldviews within a community and the presence of cultural constructs such as religious narratives, folklore, and societal norms. Individuals within a culture have their perceptions and interpretations of the world shaped by the beliefs that they hold in common.

Cultural relativism and the concept of divergent realities: Cultural relativism recognizes that beliefs and perceptions are dependent on the context in which they are held and that they differ from culture to culture. Something that one culture considers to be a spiritual experience may be interpreted as a psychological phenomenon by another culture.

The malleability and subjectivity of perception are brought into sharper focus by the fact that different cultural frameworks produce contrasting realities.

Both societal expectations and social norms play a role in the formation of beliefs that influence perception. These two factors also contribute to the formation of beliefs. When individuals conform to the accepted norms of a society, it can result in the formation of shared expectations, which in turn shapes how individuals perceive both themselves and others. The way people perceive and evaluate things can change in response to deviations from the norms of society.

The Placebo Effect: Making Beliefs Work in Practice

Physiological Responses and the Placebo Effect The placebo effect is a remarkable example of how belief can directly influence physiological responses. Individuals may experience a response from their bodies as if the treatment is effective when they have the belief that they are receiving a treatment that is beneficial, even if the treatment is passive. The power of belief is demonstrated by this phenomenon, which demonstrates that the mind has the ability to influence the functioning of the body.

Neurobiological Mechanisms: Neurobiological mechanisms underpin the placebo effect, involving the release of neurotransmitters and the modulation of pain perception. It is a demonstration of the intricate connection that exists between mental states and physical experiences that the brain is triggered to produce endorphins and other chemicals when it is convinced that a treatment is effective. These chemicals contribute to the positive outcomes that have been reported.

Beliefs and perceptions that are unfavorable caused by the placebo effect

On the other hand, the nocebo effect emphasizes the influence that negative beliefs have on perception as well as the outcomes of health activities. When individuals anticipate unfavorable outcomes, their bodies may react in a manner that is consistent with their expectations, which may result in the manifestation of symptoms or adverse effects. By highlighting the role that belief plays in shaping not only positive but also negative outcomes, the nocebo effect highlights the importance of belief.

Regarding the Paranormal, Expectations and Perceptions

Belief in the Supernatural: The belief in the supernatural offers a compelling context for investigating the dynamic relationship between perception and expectation. There is a possibility that people who have strong beliefs in ghosts, spirits, or other paranormal phenomena are more likely to interpret ambiguous stimuli as evidence of the supernatural. Convictions that are cultural, religious, or personal can have an effect on how individuals perceive and explain experiences that are beyond their comprehension.

The perception of haunting phenomena is heavily influenced by one's expectations, which play a significant role in the experience of these phenomena. It is possible for people who have a predisposition to believe in ghosts to interpret ordinary sounds, shadows, or fluctuations in the environment as evidence of spectral activity in places that are said to be haunted. There is a correlation between the power of belief and the subjective experience of encounters with the paranormal.

Cognitive Biases in Paranormal Investigations Confirmation bias and expectancy bias are two examples of cognitive biases that are frequently encountered in the field of paranormal investigations. Those who are conducting investigations with the expectation of coming across ghosts may consider ambiguous stimuli, such as electronic voice phenomena (EVP) or anomalous readings on ghost-hunting equipment, to be evidence that supports their expectations. These biases are a factor that contributes to the support of beliefs regarding the supernatural.

Personalized anticipations and the phenomenon of self-fulfilling prophecies

Self-Fulfilling Prophecies: Personal expectations have the potential to become self-fulfilling prophecies, which involve the influence of one's beliefs on one's behavior and the outcomes that one experiences. People have the potential to unconsciously contribute to the realization of a particular outcome by the actions and perceptions they take when they have a specific expectation of that outcome. This psychological phenomenon highlights the powerful role that belief plays in shaping an individual's experience of the world.

Beliefs have the ability to influence psychosomatic responses, which are the physiological manifestations of mental states that have an effect on physical health. For instance, people who anticipate experiencing stress or anxiety may discover that they are experiencing physical symptoms, such as headaches or digestive problems. The connection between the mind and the body demonstrates how beliefs can play a role in the manifestation of physiological responses.

Success in one's professional life and in one's educational pursuits are examples of personal expectations that extend to long-term objectives and accomplishments. It is possible for people who have expectations of academic excellence or professional success to exhibit behaviors and make decisions that are in line with those expectations. Belief plays a significant role in the formation of life trajectories, as evidenced by the fact that it has an impact on motivation, persistence, and decision-making.

Overcoming Unfavorable Beliefs and Taking Advantage of Positive Expectations

Both cognitive restructuring techniques and mindfulness practices provide avenues for overcoming negative beliefs and promoting positive expectations. Mindfulness practices and cognitive restructuring techniques are two examples of these activities. It is possible for individuals to change their perceptions and responses to a variety of situations by challenging and reframing negative thought patterns. Individuals are able to approach experiences with a clearer and more balanced mindset when they engage in mindfulness practices, which cultivate awareness.

The role of positive affirmations Positive affirmations, which are statements that are repeated in order to reinforce positive beliefs, can play a role in the development of a positive mindset. Positive affirmations have the ability to influence the subconscious mind, thereby molding perceptions and bolstering a constructive internal dialogue. The incorporation of positive affirmations into one's daily routines has the potential to contribute to a more optimistic outlook.

Utilizing the Placebo Effect to Improve Well-Being Individuals can gain valuable insights into how they can utilize the power of belief to improve their well-being by gaining an understanding of the placebo effect. Individuals have the ability to influence their physiological responses by cultivating positive beliefs about health and recovery. To demonstrate the potential of a holistic approach to health and healing, it is important to incorporate treatments that are based on evidence alongside those that are based on beliefs.

The intricate dance that takes place between perception and belief sheds light on the profound impact that cognitive frameworks have on the construction of how reality is perceived. Individuals are able to interpret and make sense of their experiences through the lens of their expectations, which can be shaped by a variety of factors, including cultural, societal, or personal influences. In addition to having an effect on physiological responses, self-fulfilling prophecies, and long-term accomplishments, the power of belief extends beyond the realm of subjective perception.

As we move through the terrain of perception and belief, it becomes abundantly clear that the cultivation of awareness of our expectations and beliefs is absolutely necessary in order to cultivate a more intentional and mindful approach to life. Understanding the power of belief provides a transformative perspective on the dynamic interplay between the mind and reality, which can be applied to a variety of endeavors, including the pursuit of personal goals, the management of health and well-being, and the investigation of the paranormal. Individuals are able to navigate the intricate tapestry of their beliefs, shape their perceptions, and cultivate a more meaningful and purposeful experience of the world when they embrace this awareness.

5.2 Shared Experiences: Group dynamics and the amplification of encounters

The dynamics of the groups to which we belong have a significant impact on the experiences that we have as individuals; these experiences are not isolated occurrences. The collective nature of group dynamics plays a significant role in shaping and amplifying these experiences, whether they are shared moments of joy, difficulty, or, intriguingly, encounters with the extraordinary. This is true regardless of the type of experience that is being discussed. The purpose of this investigation is to investigate the complex relationship that exists between group dynamics and shared experiences. As part of this investigation, we will investigate how the presence of a collective affects the perception, interpretation, and intensity of extraordinary occurrences.

The Connections That Are Made Through Human Experience

The significance of shared experiences lies in the fact that human beings are inherently social creatures, and the act of sharing experiences is deeply ingrained in our nature. Within a group, a sense of connection, belonging, and shared identity can be fostered through the presence of shared experiences. It doesn't matter if we're talking about families, communities, or larger societies; the collective nature of human existence is characterized by the sharing of moments that shape our understanding of the world.

The influence of the group on perception The dynamics of the group have a significant influence on the perceptions of individuals. When individuals are in the presence of other people, it can shape how they interpret events, which in turn can influence their feelings, judgments, and responses. Through the use of this collective lens, the significance and emotional resonance of experiences are frequently amplified, which contributes to the collective construction of meaning that occurs within a group.

Validation from Others and a Sense of Belonging: The experiences that people have in common serve as a source of social validation and help to reinforce emotions of belonging. When people in a group have experiences that they have in common, it helps to strengthen social bonds and affirms the beliefs and values that are held in common by the group. Individuals' approaches to and interpretations of their experiences are significantly impacted by the desire to be validated and connected within a group setting.

The dynamics of groups and the amplification of extraordinary encounters with other people

Group Attention and Awareness: When a group focuses its collective attention on a specific phenomenon or event, the shared focus heightens the perception of that experience. This is where collective attention and awareness come into play.

The heightened awareness that exists within the group has the potential to magnify the significance of encounters, making them more prominent and memorable for individuals who take part in or witness the event.

Emotional Contagion: Emotional contagion is a phenomenon that is characteristic of group dynamics. This phenomenon manifests itself when the feelings of a single individual can quickly spread throughout a group. It is possible for the emotional responses of one person to influence the emotional responses of other people in the context of shared encounters. This can result in the creation of a shared emotional atmosphere that amplifies the overall impact of the experience.

Confirmation Bias and Groupthink: The dynamics of a group can play a role in the development of confirmation bias and groupthink, which involves the tendency of individuals within a group to conform to the beliefs and perspectives that are held in common by the group. It is possible for a shared narrative to emerge as a result of the collective reinforcement of particular interpretations or explanations in the context of extraordinary encounters. This narrative serves to reinforce the perceived significance of the event.

Collective Witnessing and the Otherworldly

Group Witnessing of Paranormal Phenomena: Group witnessing is a common occurrence in the realm of paranormal encounters. This refers to the phenomenon in which multiple individuals simultaneously experience or observe the same phenomenon. There are additional layers of complexity that are added to the interpretation and validation of the encounter due to the fact that these experiences are shared. There is a correlation between the dynamics of the group and the collective construction of meaning and comprehension of the supernatural occurrence.

Intensification of Perceived Anomalies The presence of a group has the potential to amplify the perceived anomalies that are associated with encounters with the paranormal. It is possible that something that an individual might consider to be ambiguous or subtle will become more pronounced and validated when it is discussed among a group of people. A narrative that emphasizes the supernatural quality of the experience is developed as a result of this collective amplification, which contributes to the development of the narrative.

The impact of culture on the interpretation of paranormal events is significant because cultural factors play a significant role in determining how paranormal experiences are interpreted within a group structure.

The framework that individuals within a group use to interpret and make sense of extraordinary events is influenced by the cultural beliefs, folklore, and mythologies that are understood by all members of the group. Cultural resonance among the members of the group contributes to an increase in the overall significance of the paranormal encounter.

Interactions That Have Been Shared Within the Context of History and Culture

Mythologies of History and Culture: Throughout the course of human history, shared experiences have been an essential component in the development of cultural mythologies. Frequently, the stories that are told about miraculous occurrences, heavenly phenomena, or encounters with supernatural beings originate from the collective experiences that occur within communities. Eventually, these narratives that are shared become an essential component of cultural identity and belief systems.

Spiritual Experiences and Religious Gatherings: Religious and spiritual gatherings are a prime example of the power that can be harnessed through the sharing of experiences within the context of the extraordinary. A common component of collective worship, rituals, and ceremonies is the anticipation of encounters with the divine or experiences that transcend conventional boundaries. For the purpose of amplification and validation of spiritual encounters, the group dynamics that occur within religious contexts are a significant contributor.

Stories of shared encounters with mythical creatures, ghosts, and other supernatural entities are abundant in folklore and legends. Folklore and legends are replete with such stories. In many cases, these narratives originate from the collective experiences that occur within communities and are then handed down from generation to generation. As a result of the communal sharing of these stories, cultural beliefs are strengthened, and a collective framework for comprehending the mystery is provided within the community.

Investigations of the Group and Research Concerning the Paranormal

Investigations of the Paranormal and the Effects of Group Dynamics Paranormal investigators frequently work together in groups in order to investigate and record extraordinary occurrences. The dynamics of the group within the context of paranormal investigations have an effect on how individuals interpret and react to the possibility of future encounters. Sharing a common interest in the supernatural helps to cultivate a collective mindset that has the potential to contribute to the amplification and validation of phenomena that have been reported.

Technology plays a significant role in group investigations. For example, digital recording devices and ghost-hunting equipment are examples of technological advancements that are frequently utilized in group investigations investigating the paranormal. It is possible for the presence of technology within a group to enhance the perception of paranormal activity.

This is because the presence of shared readings, recordings, and visual evidence contributes to the collective validation of the experienced phenomenon.

Challenges Presented by Group Dynamics in Paranormal Research Although group dynamics have the potential to heighten the intensity of shared experiences, they also present difficult challenges in the field of paranormal research. There is a possibility that the objectivity of investigations could be affected by factors such as groupthink, confirmation bias, and the influence of dominant personalities within the group. When it comes to protecting the credibility of paranormal research, it is essential to find a middle ground between the pursuit of collective exploration and the maintenance of an approach that is both critical and open-minded.

The impact of the media and popular culture on everyday life

Representations of Shared Paranormal Encounters in the Media The media, which includes movies, television shows, and content found online, frequently depicts shared paranormal encounters. The representations in question contribute to the expectations of society and help shape the cultural beliefs that are associated with the supernatural. The way in which individuals within a group approach and interpret their own experiences is influenced by the collective consumption of narratives from the media.

Pop culture and urban legends: Most of the time, urban legends and pop culture phenomena are the result of people getting together and telling stories to one another. These shared narratives become woven into the fabric of popular belief, regardless of whether they are fueled by content that goes viral on the internet or by word-of-mouth communications. The widespread dissemination of urban legends is a factor that contributes to the amplification and continuation of extraordinary stories.

Social Media and Online Communities: The proliferation of social media has been a game-changer in terms of how people communicate their experiences with the supernatural. People are able to share their experiences, discuss their interpretations, and look for validation within a global context through the use of online communities, which provide platforms for these activities. Because of the collective nature of these online spaces, they contribute to the amplification and dissemination of narratives that are commonly associated with the paranormal.

Experiences that are shared, particularly those that are of an extraordinary nature, weave a collective tapestry that reflects the complexities of human connection and interpretation. Individuals' perceptions and interpretations of encounters, whether they are spiritual, culturally significant, or paranormal, are significantly impacted by the dynamics of the group in which they find themselves.

In order to successfully navigate this collective tapestry of experience, it is of the utmost importance to acknowledge the significant influence that group dynamics have on the amplification, validation, and interpretation of experiences that are shared.

When individuals within a group interact with one another, it increases the level of depth and nuance that we have in our understanding of the extraordinary. Whether it be through the exploration of the paranormal, the participation in cultural rituals, or the participation in the collective narratives of history, the dynamics of human connection shape the significance and the lasting impact of experiences that you share with other people. We are able to gain insights into the rich and complex tapestry of human experience when we acknowledge the power of group dynamics. This is because the extraordinary becomes a shared thread that binds us together in the vast fabric of existence.

5.3 Psychological Explanations: Sleep paralysis, hallucinations, and ghostly illusions

There is a thin veil that separates wakefulness and sleep, and this thin veil frequently gives rise to experiences that are mysterious and unsettling. These experiences can wrongly be interpreted as encounters with the supernatural. There is a triad of psychological phenomena that, when combined, can produce vivid and eerie perceptions. These phenomena are sleep paralysis, hallucinations, and ghostly illusions. The purpose of this investigation is to delve into the complex web of psychological explanations that lie behind these phenomena, thereby elucidating the mysteries that frequently accompany the realms of the mind during sleep and wakefulness.

A Concise Investigation of Sleep Partial Paralysis

Sleep paralysis is a condition that occurs during the transition between wakefulness and sleep, typically during the rapid eye movement (REM) stage of sleep. The physiology of sleep paralysis is described and explained below. The body goes through a period of temporary paralysis, which is a protective mechanism that prevents individuals from physically acting out their dreams. On the other hand, sleep paralysis occurs when consciousness becomes partially or fully active during this phase. This causes individuals to be temporarily unable to move or speak.

Hallucinations of the senses that occur during sleep paralysis Sleep paralysis is frequently accompanied by vivid sensory hallucinations. In addition to the sensation of pressure on the chest, auditory hallucinations, and most notably, visual hallucinations of shadowy figures or apparitions, these hallucinations can manifest themselves in a variety of different ways. When paralysis is combined with hallucinations, the result can be an experience that is extremely surreal and frequently terrifying.

Perspectives from Culture and History Sleep paralysis has been interpreted in a variety of ways throughout history and across cultures. These interpretations have been influenced by a wide range of cultural and supernatural beliefs. Many stories about nocturnal spirits, demonic visitations, and alien abductions have their origins in the experiences of people who have experienced sleep paralysis on multiple occasions. The cultural narratives that surround these occurrences can be made more understandable by gaining an understanding of the psychological basis of these events.

On the other hand, hallucinations are a window into the mind of Dreamers

When it comes to hallucinations, the brain plays a significant role. Hallucinations, which are defined as the perception of stimuli that are not present, can occur across a variety of sensory modalities. During the stages of sleep and wakefulness, hallucinations frequently manifest themselves as a result of abnormalities in the activity of the brain. The occurrence of hallucinatory experiences is influenced by factors such as abnormalities in the release of neurotransmitters, the processing of sensory information, and the regulation of consciousness.

Pareidolia and Visual Hallucinations: The phenomenon of pareidolia can provide an explanation for visual hallucinations, including those that are frequently associated with encounters with ghosts. The behavior known as pareidolia occurs when the brain has a tendency to recognize familiar patterns, such as faces or figures, in stimuli that are random or ambiguous. This tendency can lead to the misperception of ordinary objects as supernatural entities, particularly when they are in low-light conditions or when the individual is experiencing heightened emotional states.

Cognitive Biases and Interpretations: The interpretation of hallucinatory experiences is significantly influenced by cognitive biases, such as confirmation bias and expectancy bias. These biases play a significant role in shaping the behavior of individuals. It's possible that people who have preconceived notions about the supernatural or who are preoccupied with the idea of ghostly encounters are more likely to interpret ambiguous stimuli as evidence of the presence of the supernatural within their environment.

Spectral illusions: bridging the gap between sleep and wakefulness

The Hypnagogic and Hypnopompic Hallucinations That Are Associated with Sleep:

There is a possibility that ghostly illusions are caused by sleep-related hallucinations that occur during the transitional states of hypnagogia (the process of falling asleep) and hypnopompic (the process of waking up). The vivid sensory experiences that are characteristic of these hallucinations include both visual and auditory components, and they are frequently influenced by imagery that is similar to that of a dream. Due to the fact that the boundaries between the dream world and wakefulness are often unclear, people may experience perceptions that are similar to those of paranormal encounters.

Hypnagogic Jerk and Startle Reflex: The hypnagogic jerk, which is an involuntary muscle contraction that occurs as individuals are falling asleep, can contribute to the perception of ghostly encounters. The startle reflex is another factor that can contribute to seeing ghosts. Individuals are startled by this sudden movement, which is frequently accompanied by a feeling of falling, and it has the potential to cause either auditory or visual hallucinations. There is a possibility that the incorporation of these sensations into the developing dream state will result in the formation of spectral representations.

The interpretation of ghostly illusions is influenced by cultural beliefs and expectations, which can lead to variations in how ghostly perceptions are perceived by different cultures. Individuals may be more likely to interpret ambiguous sensory experiences as interactions with spirits in cultures where ghostly encounters are deeply ingrained in folklore or religious narratives. This is because these cultures have a greater culture of ghosts. Variations in culture are a contributing factor to the wide range of ghostly encounters that have been reported.

Behavioral Disorders, Hallucinations, and Cultural Beliefs

Cultural Frameworks and Supernatural Interpretations: Sleep paralysis and hallucinations are frequently interpreted by individuals through the lens of their cultural frameworks and belief systems. It is possible that people who have experienced sleep paralysis may attribute their experiences to malevolent spirits, witches, or other supernatural entities in societies where supernatural explanations are prevalent. The mutually beneficial relationship that exists between psychology and culture is brought into focus by the fact that cultural narratives have an impact on how these phenomena are interpreted.

In the context of religious and spiritual beliefs, the interpretation of sleep paralysis and hallucinations is significantly influenced by the religious and spiritual beliefs that are held. The experiences may be interpreted as spiritual visitations, encounters with divine beings, or confrontations with malevolent forces, depending on the variety of faith traditions that are being discussed. The cultural understanding of these experiences is made more complicated by the intersection of psychological phenomena and religious beliefs, which adds layers of complexity.

The Influence of the Media and Popular Culture The depictions of supernatural encounters in the media, such as depictions of ghosts and other malevolent entities, can play a role in the interpretation of sleep-related phenomena. The cultural narratives surrounding sleep paralysis and hallucinations are further shaped by the fact that individuals who are exposed to sensationalized representations in movies, television shows, or online content may incorporate these themes into their own experiences.

Methods for Dealing with Sleep-Related Uncertainties

Understanding Sleep-Related Experiences It is essential to educate individuals about the psychological foundations of sleep paralysis, hallucinations, and ghostly illusions in order to remove the mystery surrounding these phenomena. Individuals are better able to contextualize their experiences within a scientific framework when they are provided with information regarding the physiology of sleep and the commonality of such experiences.

Improving Mental Health Sleep-related phenomena can be upsetting, especially when they are accompanied by fear or anxiety. Here are some ways to improve mental health. In order to promote mental well-being, it is necessary to address the emotional impact that these experiences have provided. Supporting individuals who experience sleep-related phenomena, reducing the stigma associated with them, and encouraging open communication are all factors that contribute to the overall mental health of these individuals.

Seeking Professional Guidance It is recommended that individuals seek professional guidance in situations where sleep-related phenomena have a significant impact on the well-being of the individual. Sleep specialists, psychologists, or therapists who have expertise in sleep disorders are able to provide individualized interventions to address sleep-related issues and the psychological distress that is associated with them.

Recent Developments in Sleep Research The ongoing developments in sleep research continue to shed light on the complexities of sleep-related phenomena. An improved understanding of the neurobiological mechanisms that underlie sleep paralysis, hallucinations, and other experiences that are related to these conditions contributes to the development of more targeted interventions and treatments for individuals who may be adversely affected by these phenomena.

Studies Conducted Across Cultures: Studies conducted across cultures that investigate the prevalence and interpretation of sleep-related phenomena can provide valuable insights into the cultural differences in perceptions and beliefs. By conducting research that compares different societies, we are able to gain a better understanding of how the cultural context influences the subjective experience of encounters that are related to sleep experiences.

A Holistic Approach to Understanding and Treating Sleep-Related Phenomena The integration of psychological perspectives with sleep medicine helps to foster a holistic approach to understanding and treating sleep-related phenomena. By working together, researchers, psychologists, and sleep specialists can contribute to the development of comprehensive approaches that take into account the psychological as well as the physiological aspects of these experiences.

Psychological experiences that bridge the realms of sleep and wakefulness include sleep paralysis, hallucinations, and ghostly illusions. These experiences form a tapestry of psychological experiences. An understanding of the fascinating relationship that exists between the mind, cultural beliefs, and the mysteries of the night can be gained through the process of unraveling the intricate threads that make up these phenomena. A nuanced understanding that incorporates psychology, sleep science, and cultural awareness is required because the lines between the ordinary and the extraordinary are becoming increasingly blurry. This reveals the remarkable capabilities of the mind and highlights the necessity of these capabilities. As our investigation into the realms of the mind continues, the tapestry of sleep-related phenomena transforms into a canvas where science, culture, and individual experiences intersect. This canvas invites us to navigate the complex landscapes of the unconscious mind.

Chapter 6

Unraveling Mysteries

The human imagination has always been captivated by mysteries, which has led to exploration, inquiry, and an unending search for comprehension that has never been satisfied. We are beckoned to discover the mysteries that lie within the unknown, which range from the mysterious depths of the cosmos to the mysteries that are buried deep within the human mind. The purpose of this in-depth investigation is to investigate the scientific, historical, and cultural aspects that define our pursuit of knowledge and the profound allure of the unexplained. This investigation delves into the multifaceted realms of mysteries.

The Mystery of the Universe: Revealing the Hidden Truths of Being in the Universe

Dark Matter and Dark Energy: Shadows Created by the Universe

Our fundamental understanding of the universe is challenged by the mysteries that are hidden within the vastness and incomprehensibility of the cosmos it contains. However, despite the fact that they make up a sizeable portion of the universe, dark matter and dark energy continue to be evasive and difficult to detect using conventional methods. Unraveling the nature of these cosmic shadows is one of the most important challenges that contemporary astrophysics is currently facing.

The Black Hole Paradox: The Unyielding Hold of Gravity to the Universe

There is a paradox at the core of our understanding of physics that is presented by black holes, which are celestial entities that possess gravitational forces that are so powerful that not even light can escape their grasp. In the process of investigating the event horizon and singularity of black holes, mysteries are revealed that present a challenge to our comprehension of space, time, and the very fabric of the universe.

The search for extraterrestrial life and the discovery of extrasolar planets: a cosmic quest

The discovery of extrasolar planets, also known as exoplanets, has sparked a renewed interest in the search for life beyond our solar system. Unraveling the mysteries of habitable zones, biosignatures, and the possibility of life beyond Earth opens up new frontiers in the field of astrobiology and raises existential questions about the place of humanity in the universe.

The Mysterious Past: Exploring the Fabric of Time and History

Ancient Civilizations and the Knowledge That Has Been Lost: Reverberations of Antiquity

The remnants of ancient civilizations, which are characterized by architectural marvels and mysterious artifacts, contain stories of human ingenuity and knowledge that have not been related to future generations. A deeper understanding of human history and the development of societies can be attained through the process of unraveling the mysteries of ancient cultures. Some examples of these mysteries include the construction of the pyramids and the deciphering of ancient scripts.

Cryptic whispers from the past are contained within the Voynich Manuscript.

The Voynich Manuscript, which is an ancient text written in a script that is unknown and adorned with illustrations that are mysterious, continues to be a mystery that has not been solved. As time goes on, historians, cryptographers, and academics continue to decipher the secrets that are encoded within its pages. These secrets provide glimpses into a bygone era and the complexities of deciphering languages that have been lost.

Disappearances and unexplained events throughout history present a number of mysteries

Unfathomable occurrences and incidents of disappearance have left indelible marks on the historical record throughout the course of human history. Ongoing investigations and speculations are being conducted as a result of the fact that the fate of historical figures such as Amelia Earhart, the mystery of the Mary Celeste, and the enigma of the Roanoke Colony continue to elude definitive explanations.

The Cognitive Puzzle: Finding Your Way Through the Depths of Your Mind

The Inner Sanctum and Your Consciousness in Relation to the Difficult Problem

The nature of consciousness, which can be defined as the subjective experience of awareness and selfhood, is a profound mystery that is frequently referred to as the "hard problem." Exploring the neural correlates, subjective states, and philosophical underpinnings that define our inner sanctum of experience is a necessary step in the process of unraveling the complexities of consciousness.

The theater of the night is composed of fantasies and the unconscious.

Dreams, which are a nightly journey into the surreal landscapes of the unconscious mind, present a psychological mystery that has fascinated thinkers throughout the course of human history. By deciphering the meanings, functions, and neuroscientific foundations of dreams, one can gain a better understanding of the mysteries that occur in the mind while one is sleeping.

The Mystery of Mental Health and the Problems Caused by Psychological Disorders:

Researchers continue to work toward a better understanding of the biological, environmental, and genetic factors that contribute to conditions such as schizophrenia, bipolar disorder, and depression. However, the complexities of mental health and psychological disorders continue to be a significant mystery. The advancement of treatments and the reduction of stigma associated with mental health issues are both dependent on the unraveling of the mysteries of the mind.

The Cultural Tapestry: Myths, Legends, and Supernatural Intrigues is the fourth section.

Cryptids and other mythical creatures, also known as folklore creatures:

There are numerous stories of cryptids and other mythical creatures that can be found in folklore and legends. These include the Chupacabra and the Loch Ness Monster. The human fascination with the unknown and the symbolic significance of mythical entities can be better understood by deciphering the cultural origins of these stories as well as the psychological foundations upon which they are based.

The Mystical Realms of Worship, Including Sacred Sites and Rituals

The mystical allure of sacred sites and rituals across cultures is primarily due to the fact that they are shrouded in the mysteries of religious and spiritual practices. Unraveling the significance of these sacred spaces and the rituals that are performed within them reveals the myriad of ways in which people try to establish a connection with the divine and the transcendent.

Scripts from the past and unsolved codes are examples of cultural mysteries

The unsolved codes, ancient scripts, and symbolic systems that have been left behind by cultures all over the world continue to be a source of consternation for researchers. Deciphering these cultural mysteries, which range from the script used in the Indus Valley to the Rongorongo script used on Easter Island, contributes to our understanding of the relationship between linguistic evolution and cultural exchange.

Quantum quirks and unanswered questions are the subject of scientific enigma

Quantum Entanglement: Spooky Action at a Distance: Quantum entanglement, a phenomenon described by Einstein as "spooky action at a distance," challenges our classical understanding of physics. By unraveling the mysteries of entanglement and the implications for quantum mechanics, we are able to gain a deeper understanding of the fundamental nature of particles and the fabric of reality.

The Characteristics of Dark Energy and Dark Matter Regarding the Persistence of Cosmic Shadows

Despite the fact that dark energy and dark matter are essential to our comprehension of the universe, they continue to evade direct detection and comprehension among scientists. Investigating the nature of these cosmic shadows requires ongoing research in the fields of cosmology, particle physics, and astrophysics in order to determine the role that these shadows play in the formation of the universe.

When it comes to the search for unity, the Grand Unified Theory

In the realm of theoretical physics, the pursuit of a Grand Unified Theory (GUT) that represents the unification of the fundamental forces of nature continues to be an intriguing challenge. When the mysteries of quantum mechanics and general relativity are unraveled at a fundamental level, there is the possibility that a unified understanding of the principles that govern the universe will be revealed.

The Ethical Mystery: Finding Your Way Through Moral Conundrums and Conundrums

In the field of science and technology, ethical dilemmas can be found in dystopian futures.

The advancement of science and technology has resulted in the emergence of ethical conundrums that require extensive consideration. In order to unravel the ethical implications of emerging technologies, genetic engineering, and artificial intelligence, it is necessary to conduct a careful investigation of the potential consequences and to exercise responsible stewardship of innovation.

A Look at the Moral Ambiguities in History: Unraveling the Threads of Injustice Historical events frequently give rise to moral questions concerning justice, accountability, and restitution. In order to unravel the threads of injustice, such as those that were woven into the fabric of colonialism, slavery, and systemic oppression, it is necessary to engage in ethical reflection and to make a commitment to addressing the lingering consequences of past transgressions.

The sustainability of human existence on Earth presents an ethical mystery that is intertwined with environmental considerations. Environmental ethics and the mystery of sustainable coexistence present a challenge to the sustainability of human existence. In order to unravel the complexities of environmental ethics, it is necessary to navigate the delicate balance that exists between human needs, the preservation of biodiversity, and the responsible stewardship of the planet for future generations.

Mysteries, which are woven into the grand tapestry of existence, invite us to venture into the uncharted territories of both the known and the unknown.

The pursuit of unraveling mysteries is an endeavor that transcends boundaries and has stood the test of time. Whether we are looking into the depths of the cosmos, sifting through the annals of history, navigating the complexities of the human mind, or grappling with ethical dilemmas, the exploration of mysteries is an endeavor that transcends boundaries.

As we delve deeper into the mysteries that surround us, it becomes abundantly clear that the journey of unraveling mysteries is not only about the answers that we seek, but also about the questions that we ask along the way. A spirit of curiosity, humility, and awe is fostered when we invite ourselves to embrace the unknown, which in turn invites us to continue our pursuit of knowledge and comprehension. The mysteries that continue to exist in the fields of science, history, culture, and ethics serve as invitations to engage in an ongoing exploration of the complexity and interconnectedness of the various aspects of the universe. Within the context of this ongoing journey, the unraveling of mysteries becomes a demonstration of the tenacity of human curiosity and the boundless possibilities that are waiting for those who have the courage to venture into the realms of the unknown.

6.1 In-Depth Investigations: Examining famous haunted locations

People who are looking for thrills, people who are interested in paranormal investigations, and people who are curious about the mysteries that surround haunted locations have been drawn to these locations for a long time because they are a source of fascination. There are a variety of famous haunted locations that have captured the imaginations of people all over the world. These locations range from abandoned asylums and lighthouses to historic mansions and ancient castles. The purpose of this investigation is to delve into in-depth investigations of some of the most notorious haunted sites, revealing the historical context, the reported paranormal activity, and the scientific scrutiny that seeks to explain the unexplained.

The Tower of London, an intriguing mystery from antiquity

The Tower of London is a well-known landmark that depicts the rich history of England, which dates back to the Norman Conquest in 1066. It is considered to be an iconic symbol of England's rich history. The Tower, which was initially constructed as a fortress and ultimately expanded into a royal palace and prison, has been the site of political intrigue, royal drama, and executions over the course of several centuries.

Reports of paranormal activity at the Tower of London include sightings of apparitions, ghostly figures, and mysterious sounds. These reports have been made public. It is said that the White Tower, which is the oldest part of the complex, is haunted by the ghosts of historical figures such as Anne Boleyn, Lady Jane Grey, and others who met their tragic end within its walls.

In-Depth Investigations: In order to conduct in-depth investigations into the paranormal at the Tower of London, electromagnetic field (EMF) meters, infrared cameras, and audio recording devices have been utilized. The objective of the researchers is to validate the reported encounters with ghosts by using scientific methods and to collect evidence of ghostly phenomena. On the other hand, the presence of multiple historical layers and the cultural significance of the location make it difficult to differentiate between fact and folklore.

The Gothic Mystery: The Winchester Mystery House

The Winchester Mystery House, which can be found in San Jose, California, is a well-known architectural oddity that is renowned for its labyrinthine design and peculiar architectural features. The mansion was constructed by Sarah Winchester, who was the widow of the man who invented the famous rifle. The construction process lasted for almost forty years and was continuously ongoing. The sprawling structure features doors that open into walls, staircases that lead nowhere, and a labyrinth of corridors that are difficult to understand for the average person.

There are a number of legends and lore that surround the Winchester Mystery House. One of these legends suggests that Sarah Winchester, who was driven by guilt and a belief in the supernatural, constructed the mansion in order to appease the spirits of those who had been killed from Winchester rifles. It is said that she held séances every night in order to receive instructions from the spirits regarding how to proceed with the construction.

Investigations of the Paranormal: It has been investigated by paranormal investigators that the Winchester Mystery House has been investigated in order to find evidence to support claims of hauntings. Investigators have conducted ghost tours of the mansion, and they have utilized various tools, including infrared thermometers and EVP (Electronic Voice Phenomena) recorders, in order to document any unusual occurrences that may have taken place. It is possible that the architectural peculiarities and legends contributed to the perceptions of paranormal activity, according to those who are skeptical.

Myrtles Plantation, the Gothic Romance

To provide some historical context, the Myrtles Plantation, which can be found in St. Francisville, Louisiana, is a historic plantation in the South that has its origins dating back to the latter half of the 18th century. It is well known that the mansion is magnificent, that it is built in the antebellum style, and that it has lush gardens. Numerous historical events, including the American Civil War, have taken place in the Myrtles, which is located in South Carolina.

The Myrtles Plantation is famously considered to be one of the most haunted places in the United States of America due to its history of hauntings.

According to the urban legend, the plantation is home to a number of ghosts, some of which include Chloe, a former slave; children who died of disease; and other apparitions. The mansion has a reputation for being haunted, which has been contributed to by reports of ghostly encounters and phenomena that cannot be explained.

The Myrtles Plantation has been the site of extensive research and investigations carried out by paranormal investigators. These investigators have utilized various pieces of equipment, including electromagnetic field meters, thermal cameras, and spirit boxes, in their investigations. The purpose of this endeavor is to gather evidence of paranormal activity and verify the hauntings that have been reported. The historical significance of the location, in addition to the enduring stories of ghostly encounters, makes it an intriguing subject for investigative studies that are more in-depth.

The Asylum Anomaly, Also Known as the Trans-Allegheny Lunatic Asylum Situation

A massive Gothic building that was once used as a mental institution, the Trans-Allegheny Lunatic Asylum can be found in Weston, West Virginia. Its location is significant in terms of its historical significance. A variety of treatments, including controversial psychiatric practices of the time, were carried out at the asylum, which was constructed in the middle of the nineteenth century and continued to operate for more than a century.

The asylum is surrounded by ghostly legends and stories of tragic events that took place within its walls. These legends are said to have occurred within the asylum. A number of factors have contributed to the asylum's reputation as one of the most haunted locations in the United States. These factors include accounts of patients being mistreated, harsh conditions, and the manifestations of former inmates.

As part of the scientific investigations, the Trans-Allegheny Lunatic Asylum has been conducting paranormal investigations with the goal of documenting and analyzing the hauntings that have been reported there. In order to collect evidence, investigators make use of things like electronic voice response (EVR) recorders, full-spectrum cameras, and motion detectors. There are those who believe that the history of mental health practices at the location, as well as the atmospheric conditions of the building that is deteriorating, could be factors that contribute to the perception of paranormal activity.

The Queen Mary, the Unsolved Mysteries of Navigation

Ocean Liner Legacy: The Queen Mary, a former ocean liner that has been converted into a floating hotel in Long Beach, California, has a rich history that includes serving as a luxury cruise ship and, later, as a troop transport during World War II. The allure of the ship is enhanced by the luxurious interiors as well as the historical significance of the vessel.

Haunted Quarters: There have been numerous reports of paranormal activity aboard the Queen Mary, including sightings of apparitions, footsteps that are under mysterious circumstances, and sounds that cannot be explained. Tales of ghostly encounters in various areas of the ship have been fueled by the ship's history, which includes tragic events such as accidents and fatalities that occurred during wartime.

Research on the Paranormal: In order to investigate the alleged hauntings that have been reported, paranormal investigations have been carried out along the Queen Mary. For the purpose of documenting any irregularities, researchers make use of various pieces of equipment, including thermal imaging cameras, spirit boxes, and EMF meters. There are additional layers of complexity added to the investigation of reported paranormal phenomena as a result of the setting of the ship, which is unique and has a connection to the history of wartime and maritime tragedies.

The Castle of Edinburgh, also known as the Fortress of Shadows

Historic Stronghold: Edinburgh Castle, which is located on Castle Rock and overlooks the city of Edinburgh in Scotland, is a historic fortress that dates back to the 12th century and has a difficult and eventful history. Over the course of Scottish history, the castle has been a witness to a number of significant events, including battles, royal intrigues, and political upheavals.

Phantom Piper and Other Ghostly Legends: Edinburgh Castle is well-known for its ghostly legends, one of which is the well-known story of the Phantom Piper. As a result of the castle's reputation as one of the most haunted locations in Scotland, there have been reports of apparitions, noises that cannot be explained, and figures that appear to be ghosts. According to legend, the dungeons, the military barracks, and the ancient chapel are the locations where paranormal occurrences are most likely to occur.

Investigating the Paranormal The process of conducting paranormal investigations at Edinburgh Castle involves exploring the castle's many chambers, tunnels, and historical sites. For the purpose of gathering evidence of paranormal activity, researchers make use of a wide variety of tools, ranging from night-vision cameras to devices that facilitate communication with spirits. The castle is a compelling subject for in-depth investigations due to the fact that its history and legends are seamlessly intertwined with one another.

A rich tapestry of historical narratives, cultural beliefs, and reported paranormal phenomena is revealed when in-depth investigations of well-known haunted locations are conducted. The allure of these locations lies not only in the possibility of encounters with ghosts, but also in the layers of history and human experiences that are embedded within the walls of these locations.

The challenge of distinguishing between the genuine paranormal and the influences of history, psychology, and cultural perceptions continues to be a challenge for researchers, investigators, and enthusiasts who are navigating the shadows of the supernatural.

In the same way that haunted places act as gateways to the past, they also encourage us to investigate the mysteries that are still present within their boundaries. Individuals who conduct in-depth investigations of well-known haunted locations contribute to the ongoing investigation of the supernatural. These investigations may be motivated by a desire to gather evidence, a fascination with history, or a curiosity about unfamiliar things. During the process of uncovering the mysteries that are hidden within these locations, we continue to navigate the hazy boundaries that exist between the tangible and the ethereal, providing glimpses into the shadows of the mysteries that cannot be explained.

6.2 Witness Testimonies: Analyzing firsthand accounts

In the realm of the paranormal, witness testimonies are accounts that weave the fabric of unexplained phenomena. These accounts are intriguing and often perplexing, and they stand out as interesting accounts. The first-hand accounts of people who have had personal experiences with ghosts, unidentified flying objects (UFOs), cryptids, and other supernatural entities offer a fresh perspective through which we can observe the extraordinary. In this investigation, the complexities of witness testimonies are investigated, including the psychological foundations upon which they are based, the cultural influences that shape them, and the difficulties associated with accurately distinguishing between perception and the supernatural.

An Introduction to the Psychology of Perception: An Understanding of the Mind's Eye

Subjectivity and personal bias: Witness examinations are inherently subjective, as they are formed by the perceptions, beliefs, and cognitive processes of the individual providing the testimony. There is a significant possibility that individuals' interpretations and memories of paranormal occurrences are significantly impacted by personal bias, which is influenced by cultural background, previous experiences, and emotional states. When determining the reliability of witness accounts, it is essential to have a solid understanding of the role that subjectivity plays.

Memory, a cognitive process that is both malleable and dynamic, is an essential component of witness testimony. Reconstruction is another important aspect of memory work. Not only does the act of recalling an event involve remembering those details, but it also involves reconstructing those details. In the context of memories pertaining to paranormal experiences, the accuracy and coherence of those memories can be affected by a variety of factors, including suggestion, information obtained after the event, and the passage of time.

Cognitive Biases and Expectations: Confirmation bias and expectancy bias are two examples of cognitive biases that play a role in the formation of witness testimony. When confronted with ambiguous stimuli, individuals may unconsciously interpret them in a manner that is consistent with the beliefs or expectations they have already established. When conducting an investigation into paranormal accounts, it is essential to take into account the psychological mechanisms that are at play, as this phenomenon will demonstrate.

Cultural influences have a significant impact on the narrative of the supernatural

Cultural Beliefs and Folklore: Witness testimonies are deeply intertwined with cultural beliefs and folklore, which serve as a lens through which individuals interpret and contextualize their experiences. The perceptions that people have of ghosts, spirits, and other supernatural entities differ from culture to culture, which in turn affects how witnesses describe their experiences and how they make sense of them. Not only do cultural frameworks influence the content of paranormal events, but they also influence how significant those events are perceived to be.

Media and Popular Culture: The pervasive influence of media and popular culture is a factor that contributes to the construction of the narrative that concerns the supernatural. It is possible for individuals' expectations and interpretations of their own experiences to be influenced by depictions of ghosts, extraterrestrial beings, and other paranormal phenomena that are found in movies, television shows, and literature. In many cases, elements of cultural narratives that are perpetuated by media portrayals are reflected in the testimonies of witnesses.

Witness testimonies are not isolated phenomena; rather, they frequently emerge within social contexts. Social dynamics and group influences are important factors to consider. Both the manner in which individuals report and validate paranormal experiences can be influenced by group dynamics, shared beliefs, and collective interpretations respectively. The amplification and normalization of witness testimonies can be facilitated by social reinforcement within communities that have a positive attitude toward the supernatural.

The Different Kinds of Paranormal Encounters, Ranging from Ghosts to UFOs

Apparitions and Ghostly Encounters: Witness accounts of apparitions and ghostly encounters are commonplace across a wide range of historical periods and cultural contexts. These accounts frequently include sightings of figures that are translucent, sounds that cannot be explained, and sensations that are not typical. Pareidolia and suggestibility are two examples of psychological factors that may play a role in the interpretation of everyday stimuli as manifestations of the supernatural.

UFO Sightings and Extraterrestrial Encounters: The reports of encounters with extraterrestrial beings and sightings of unidentified flying objects (UFOs) make up a separate category of witness testimony. Descriptions of unidentified flying objects, alien abductions, and close encounters are frequently included in the narratives written by the individuals. These testimonies are shaped in significant ways by a number of factors, including the psychological impact of media depictions, the cultural expectations of the audience, and the possibility of incorrectly identifying conventional objects.

Cryptid Encounters: Encounters with Mythical and Folklore Creatures:

According to the testimonies of witnesses, cryptid encounters involve sightings of legendary or mythical creatures. Some examples of these creatures include Bigfoot, the Loch Ness Monster, and the Chupacabra. There are a number of factors that contribute to the development of these narratives, including cultural beliefs, folklore, and the human tendency to discover patterns in nature. Critiquing cryptid testimonies in an objective manner is made more difficult by the fact that the line between folklore and eyewitness accounts is increasingly blurry.

The Obstacles That Come With Examining the Testimonies of Witnesses

Memory Distortion and Reliability: Given the way in which human memory is susceptible to distortion, the reliability of witness testimonies continues to be a persistent challenge. The accuracy of recall can be impacted by a variety of factors, including stress, fear, and emotional arousal, which can occur during paranormal experiences. For researchers, the task of distinguishing between genuine experiences and memory confabulation or false memories is a challenging and difficult mission.

The function of suggestion Suggestion, whether it is made intentionally or unintentionally, has the potential to significantly impact the testimony of witnesses. There are a number of factors that can influence the way individuals articulate their experiences, including leading questions, media depictions, and the influence of investigators. When it comes to distinguishing between information that witnesses have genuinely recalled and elements that have been introduced through suggestion, the challenge remains.

Skepticism and Credibility: Witness testimonies are frequently subjected to scrutiny, including scrutiny from believers who are eager to validate supernatural narratives as well as from skeptics who are looking for rational explanations. In order to successfully navigate the complexities of witness accounts, it is essential to strike a balance between conducting inquiries with an open mind and conducting critical evaluations. Skepticism is a way of thinking that encourages a thorough investigation of alternative explanations without minimizing the significance of the experiences that are being reported.

The Scientific Methods Used in Recent Developments in the Field of Paranormal Research

Parapsychology and Experimental Investigations: Parapsychology, which is the scientific study of paranormal phenomena, makes use of experimental methodologies in order to investigate the testimonies of witnesses. Studies that are controlled, such as those involving telepathy or precognition, are conducted with the intention of providing empirical evidence for psi phenomena. On the other hand, the feasibility of applying experimental methods to spontaneous witness accounts is restricted due to the difficulties associated with reproducing paranormal occurrences in laboratory settings.

Monitoring and Technological Tools: Recent developments in technology have resulted in the introduction of new tools that can be used to monitor and record information regarding paranormal activity. When conducting investigations into the paranormal, it is common practice to make use of infrared cameras, electromagnetic field (EMF) meters, and audio recording devices in order to collect potential evidence. The purpose of incorporating scientific instrumentation into the analysis of witness testimony is to add an empirical layer to the assessment of the evidence.

Inter-disciplinary Methods: The importance of interdisciplinary collaboration between psychologists, anthropologists, historians, and scientists in the study of witness testimonies is becoming more and more widely acknowledged. A more comprehensive understanding of the psychological, cultural, and historical factors that influence paranormal experiences can be achieved through the integration of insights from a variety of disciplines.

Considerations of an Ethical Nature: Conducting Respectful Inquiries into Individual Experiences

Regarding the Witness: When it comes to the analysis of witness testimony, ethical considerations are of the utmost critical importance. It is of the utmost importance to show respect for the witness's point of view, including their cultural background and the personal significance of their experiences. It is essential for ethical investigation into paranormal encounters to have sensitivity to the potential impact that investigations could have on the well-being and beliefs of members of the public.

Fostering Open Dialogue: Creating a space for the respectful exchange of ideas is accomplished by encouraging open dialogue between those who are skeptical, those who believe, and witnesses. The promotion of an investigation into the paranormal that is more inclusive and nuanced can be accomplished by encouraging individuals to share their testimonies without the fear of being ridiculed or dismissed. The researchers and witnesses are able to work together more effectively when they have regular conversations.

Engagement with Communities and Education: Engaging with communities that have a cultural or historical connection to paranormal experiences requires an approach that is both thoughtful and educational. A discourse that is more informed and discriminating can be fostered through the dissemination of information regarding the psychological factors that influence witness testimonies, the role that cultural beliefs play, and the history of investigations into the paranormal beings.

The testimonies of witnesses, which are replete with the nuances of perception, memory, and cultural influences, come together to form a captivating tapestry that goes beyond the boundaries of the ordinary. In the process of navigating the veil that separates personal experiences and the supernatural, the challenge lies in approaching witness accounts with a combination of curiosity and skepticism. When we investigate the testimonies of witnesses, we are given the opportunity to unravel the mysteries of the human mind, cultural narratives, and the never-ending search for making sense of the things that cannot be explained.

In this ongoing journey, the analysis of witness testimonies serves not only as a window into the supernatural but also as a mirror reflecting the complexities of human cognition, belief systems, and the collective imagination. This is because the interpretation of witness testimonies serves as a window into the supernatural. In the process of deciphering the tapestry of paranormal experiences, the pursuit of knowledge is enriched by a balanced acknowledgment of the complexities that are inherent in the study of the extraordinary. Witness testimonies, with their inherent subjectivity and cultural nuances, invite us to explore the liminal spaces where the mysterious and the mundane converge. Testimonies from witnesses provide glimpses into the mysterious realms that continue to captivate the human spirit.

6.3 Debunking Myths: Separating fact from fiction in popular ghost stories

Ghost stories have been a time-honored and universal method of capturing the imagination of people for a very long time. These stories frequently have their origins in folklore, local legends, or personal experiences. These stories, which have been handed down from generation to generation, have the power to mold people's perceptions of the supernatural and contribute to the aura of mystery that surrounds haunted places. On the other hand, in the midst of the chilling stories, it is absolutely necessary to conduct an in-depth analysis and dispel any myths that may have been popularized by popular ghost stories. The purpose of this investigation is to differentiate between fact and fiction by revealing the truths that lie behind a number of well-known haunted stories.

The Woman in White, also known as the spectral appearance of folklore

There is a common theme that appears in ghost stories all over the world, and that is the "Woman in White."

Frequently portrayed as a spectral figure dressed in a flowing white gown, it is said that she makes her appearance on moonlit nights, haunting desolate roads or abandoned structures during these times. A number of tragic backstories are associated with these apparitions, according to local legends. These backstories include unrequited love, betrayal, or untimely death.

Dispelling the Myth: Although the Woman in White continues to be a well-known archetype in folklore, the origins of these tales can frequently be traced back to cultural motifs, shared archetypes, or even psychological phenomena. Eyewitness accounts are susceptible to being influenced by pareidolia, which is a tendency to perceive familiar patterns, such as human forms, in random stimuli such as shadows or mist. This phenomenon can occur in many instances. Acknowledging the psychological underpinnings that contribute to the creation of such ghostly figures is an important step in debunking the myth.

Hitchhiker: Legends of the Road: The Vanishing Hitchhiker

The story revolves around the Vanishing Hitchhiker, a spectral traveler who accepts a ride only to vanish during the journey. This is yet another ghost story that has stood the test of time. It is common for stories to assert that the spectral hitchhiker is a spirit that is attempting to reach a particular location or deliver a message, but ultimately disappears without a trace once it arrives at its destination.

Bringing to light the truth: despite the fact that this tale is told differently in different cultures, investigations have shown that many instances of the Vanishing Hitchhiker can be attributed to urban legends and anecdotes that have spread through word of mouth. There have been some cases that have been disproved as being a misinterpretation or an embellishment of real-life events. For example, there have been meetings with people who were stranded and later discovered alternative modes of transportation.

The Mysterious Tale of Annabelle and the Cursed Doll

Isabelle, the allegedly haunted doll that has been featured in a number of popular horror films, is based on a real-life case that was investigated by Ed and Lorraine Warren, who are both paranormal investigators. People who come into contact with the doll are said to be subjected to a variety of supernatural occurrences and misfortunes because it is said to be possessed by a malevolent spirit.

The truth is that the porcelain figure depicted in movies is not the real Annabelle; rather, the real story behind Annabelle involves a Raggedy Ann doll. Based on the findings of the investigations, it appears that the alleged hauntings were most likely the result of suggestion and the Warrens' involvement in shaping the narrative for dramatic effect.

The story exemplifies the power of storytelling as well as the blurred line that separates reality and fiction, despite the fact that the doll itself is now protected by a glass box.

The Ghostly Lady of La Llorona: An Apparition That Brings Together Different Cultures

La Llorona, also known as the weeping woman, is a spectral figure that is prominent in Hispanic folklore. This legend is shared by multiple cultures. It is said that she is a grieving mother who drowned her children and that she now wanders the riverbanks and waterways in search of her grandchildren and other children who have gone missing. There are numerous cultures each with their own version of a weeping woman who crosses national boundaries.

An examination of the myth Despite the fact that the La Llorona legend is deeply rooted in cultural traditions, its roots can be traced back to historical events such as the Spanish conquest of the Americas. La Llorona is a figure that serves as both a cautionary tale and a reflection of the fears that are prevalent in society. Understanding the cultural context in which this myth was created and recognizing the symbolic nature of the spectral apparition are both necessary steps in the analysis of this myth.

Amityville Horror: A House Shattered in Mysteries is the fifth installment.

The Haunting of 112 Ocean Avenue: The Amityville Horror is a notorious haunting case that centers on a house in Amityville, New York, where a family claimed to have experienced terrifying paranormal phenomena. The house is associated with the Amityville Horror. There were reports of visions of demonic entities, strange odors, and unsettling sounds, all of which contributed to the belief that the house was haunted.

Investigations into the Amityville Horror have revealed inconsistencies and embellishments in the accounts provided by the family. This has led to the deconstruction of the haunting. Some people have suggested that financial motivations played a role in perpetuating the haunting narrative with regard to the house, which has led to the widespread discrediting of the paranormal events that have been associated with the house. The process of disproving the Amityville Horror involves distinguishing between factual evidence and accounts that are sensationalized.

The Phantom of Hampton Court Palace, also known as The Grey Lady

Hauntings from the past: It is said that Hampton Court Palace in England is haunted by the Grey Lady, a ghostly figure that is associated with the Tudor period. The belief that the palace has a reputation for being haunted by the supernatural has been fueled by multiple reports of ghostly sightings, footsteps, and other unexplained occurrences.

It is possible that the ghostly encounters that visitors have reported at Hampton Court Palace are influenced by a combination of suggestive storytelling and the atmospheric nature of the historic site. This is because the historical context of Hampton Court Palace includes stories of royal drama, betrayal, and intrigue. When conducting an investigation into the haunting, it is important to take into consideration the inter-active relationship between historical narratives and the psychological impact of the atmosphere of the palace.

The ability to exercise skepticism is an essential instrument for distinguishing be-tween fact and fiction in the realm of ghost stories. In order to dispel the myths that surround popular haunted stories, it is necessary to conduct an in-depth analysis of the psychological, cultural, and historical elements that play a role in the formation and continuation of these stories. It is possible that genuine paranormal experiences do exist; however, in order to uncover the truth, it is necessary to acknowledge the influence of human perception, conventional storytelling practices, and societal fears.

In order to successfully navigate the realms of the supernatural, the search for truth requires a balance between an open-minded approach to inquiry and a discernment-based evaluation of the evidence. Ghost stories continue to captivate our imaginations, regardless of whether they are based on personal experiences or folklore. However, gaining an understanding of the myths that are woven into these narratives enables us to appreciate the rich tapestry of human storytelling while also demystifying the spectral shadows that linger in the corners of our collective consciousness.

Chapter 7

The Future of Paranormal Inquiry

In light of the fact that we are on the verge of technological advancements and expanding scientific knowledge, the future of paranormal investigation holds the promise of elucidating the mysteries that have captivated human curiosity for centuries. From the ancient folklore of the past to the scientific investigations of the present day, the quest to comprehend the supernatural has progressed gradually. This investigation delves into the possible paths that could be taken by paranormal research. It investigates the role that emerging technologies, interdisciplinary collaboration, and shifting paradigms could play in determining how we approach the unexplained.

Recent Developments in Technology Regarding Investigations of the Paranormal

Technologies of Sensors: The incorporation of cutting-edge sensor technologies is on the verge of bringing about a revolution in the field of paranormal investigations. The collection of tools that are available to researchers who are interested in the paranormal is constantly growing. These tools include electromagnetic field (EMF) meters and thermal imaging cameras. It is possible that in the future, developments will involve the utilization of sensors that are more sensitive and precise, with the ability to detect subtle energy fluctuations or strange environmental changes that are associated with paranormal phenomena.

Augmented and Virtual Reality: Technologies that offer immersive experiences, such as augmented reality (AR) and virtual reality (VR), have the potential to rethink the way that paranormal investigations are carried out. Through the use of augmented reality (AR), researchers have the ability to overlay historical data, witness testimonies, and environmental readings in real time, thereby providing a comprehensive view of haunted locations. Investigators might be able to recreate and analyze reported paranormal events with the help of virtual reality (VR) simulations, which would lead to a deeper understanding of the dynamics at play.

Artificial Intelligence (AI): AI has a tremendous amount of potential for analyzing the vast amounts of data that are gathered during investigations into the paranormal.

Algorithms that learn through machine learning have the ability to recognize patterns, anomalies, and correlations that may be invisible to human perception. There is a possibility that applications of artificial intelligence could improve the interpretation of audio recordings, categorize visual anomalies, and contribute to a more systematic analysis of psychic phenomena.

Technology pertaining to drones: Drones that are fitted with high-resolution cameras and sensors have the potential to revolutionize the exploration of locations that are either inaccessible or hazardous. Unmanned aerial vehicles (drones) can be utilized by paranormal investigators to conduct remote monitoring, survey vast areas, and capture aerial perspectives of haunted locations. Documenting unexplained phenomena and gaining new insights into paranormal hotspots could be made easier with the help of drone technology, which could be integrated into the system.

Interdisciplinary work and holistic approaches

Mainstream Science and Parapsychology: The future of paranormal research will involve a closer integration between mainstream scientific disciplines and the field of parapsychology, which is the scientific study of paranormal phenomena. To achieve a more rigorous and all-encompassing understanding of the role that the human mind plays in paranormal experiences, it will be beneficial to collaborate with professionals in the fields of psychology, physics, neuroscience, and other fields of expertise. In order to make significant progress in explaining and validating paranormal phenomena, it is possible that bridging the gap between parapsychological research and mainstream science will lead to breakthroughs.

Anthropology and the Context of Culture: When it comes to contextualizing paranormal experiences within cultural frameworks, anthropological perspectives will play a significant role. In the future, investigations into the supernatural should incorporate cultural anthropology in order to gain a better understanding of how perceptions of the supernatural are influenced by societal beliefs, folklore, and historical narratives. It is possible to arrive at interpretations that are more nuanced and culturally sensitive if one acknowledges the cultural context of the phenomena that have been reported.

Working Together with Historians and Archaeologists: Working together with historians and archaeologists will enrich the study of haunted locations by providing them with historical and archaeological context. The layers of history that are associated with paranormal hotspots can be unraveled in order to gain insights into the ways in which events from the past influence experiences that occur in the present. Understanding the complexities of haunted sites can be accomplished through the utilization of a holistic approach that combines the investigation of the paranormal with historical and archaeological knowledge.

Studies of Neuroscience and Consciousness: Investigating the intersection of neuroscience and paranormal inquiry opens up new avenues for the investigation of the connection between abnormal brain function and experiences that are not typical.

The neural mechanisms that are responsible for apparitions, altered states of consciousness, and the perception of paranormal phenomena may be better understood as a result of recent developments in neuroscience.

With the integration of consciousness studies and paranormal research, it may be possible to achieve a more nuanced understanding of the role that the mind plays in shaping encounters with the supernatural.

Pattern Recognition and Analytical Methods for Large Data Sets

Approaches that are driven by data: The future of paranormal investigation will involve utilizing the power of big data analytics to process and analyze the vast amounts of information that are gathered during investigations. The identification of recurrent patterns, correlations, and statistical anomalies that are associated with paranormal phenomena can be accomplished by researchers through the utilization of data-driven approaches. It is possible that the development of predictive models and classification algorithms will be aided by this shift toward a methodology that is more quantitative and analytical.

Pattern recognition in the context of paranormal occurrences Pattern recognition algorithms can be utilized to identify similarities among the various paranormal occurrences that have been reported. Researchers have the potential to discover underlying trends or recurring elements that are characteristic of particular types of paranormal phenomena by classifying and analyzing patterns in witness testimonies, environmental data, and historical context. A more organized comprehension of the myriad ways in which the supernatural can manifest itself could be achieved through the application of this methodical approach.

Participation of the Public and Citizen Science

In the future of paranormal investigation, there will be a greater emphasis placed on crowdsourced investigations, which will involve increased participation from the general public. The collective power of enthusiasts, skeptics, and curious individuals can be leveraged through citizen science initiatives, which allow for the contribution of data, the sharing of experiences, and active participation in research pertaining to the spiritual realm. It is possible that online platforms, mobile applications, and virtual communities could serve as hubs for collaborative investigations, thereby expanding the scope of paranormal investigation.

Social media platforms and reporting websites: Social media platforms and reporting websites that are specifically designed for reporting provide individuals with avenues through which they can share their experiences with the paranormal. It is possible that future investigations into the paranormal will make use of these platforms in order to collect data in real time, establish connections with witnesses, and recognize emerging patterns. Researchers are able to crowdsource information and construct a diverse database of paranormal encounters thanks to the immediacy and global reach of social media.

Educational Outreach: It is essential to ensure that the general public is equipped with the knowledge and tools necessary for conducting responsible paranormal investigation in order to cultivate a culture of informed curiosity. In addition to fostering critical thinking and encouraging a balanced approach to investigating the unexplained, educational outreach programs have the potential to alleviate the mystery surrounding the scientific procedures that are utilized in paranormal investigations. Involving members of the general public in the investigation process allows paranormal researchers to gain access to a wider range of perspectives and contributions.

Ethical Considerations in the Investigation of the Paranormal

Consent to Participate and Participant Well-Being: In order to ensure the ethical future of paranormal research, it is necessary to make a commitment to informed consent and the well-being of participants. Researchers have a responsibility to put the mental and emotional well-being of witnesses at the forefront of their concerns, taking into account the potential impact that investigations may have on individuals who share their experiences with the paranormal. It is essential to take into consideration ethical considerations that the research process be transparent, and that clear communication be provided regarding the potential consequences of participation.

Due to the fact that paranormal investigations are increasingly involving collaboration with a wide variety of communities, it is of the utmost importance to show respect for cultural sensitivities. Researchers are required to approach haunted locations with an awareness of the local beliefs, traditions, and cultural nuances that are present nearby. It is possible to cultivate a respectful and inclusive approach to the investigation of the paranormal by demonstrating sensitivity to the historical, spiritual, and cultural significance of locations.

Openness to Skepticism and Critical Inquiry: Skepticism and critical inquiry are both recognised as essential components of the scientific method, and ethical paranormal inquiry is open to both of these approaches. It is important for researchers to be open to scrutiny, to encourage diverse perspectives, and to maintain an open mind regarding alternative explanations for phenomena that have been reported. Establishing trust within the scientific community and with the general public can be accomplished through the use of transparent methodology, data collection, and analysis.

The development of paradigms: from the realm of mysticism to the realm of scientific exploration

Changing Paradigms in Paranormal Research The future of paranormal research will be marked by a paradigm shift away from mysticism and superstition and toward scientific investigation. Researchers have the ability to navigate the uncharted territories of the supernatural with rigor and methodological precision when they adopt an approach that is more empirical and evidence-based. Through this shift, the investigation of the paranormal is brought into alignment with the broader trends in scientific advancements and collaboration across disciplines.

Integration of Quantum Concepts It is possible that the investigation of quantum concepts will play a part in determining the course of developments in the field of paranormal research. The conventional ideas of space, time, and causality are being called into question by the introduction of concepts such as entanglement, non-locality, and the observer effect. Although it is speculative to apply quantum principles to paranormal phenomena, the ever-evolving understanding of quantum mechanics may have an impact on how researchers conceptualize and investigate phenomena that cannot be explained.

The development of cultural attitudes and perspectives on the supernatural:

Attitudes toward the supernatural fluctuate in tandem with the development of societies. Changing cultural norms, increased scientific literacy, and the ongoing conversation between different belief systems and empirical evidence are all factors that will have an impact on the future of paranormal research. Conversations that are open and honest about the supernatural, in conjunction with research practices that are responsible and transparent, contribute to a cultural evolution in which the unexplained is approached with curiosity rather than fear.

When it comes to the investigation of the supernatural, the future of paranormal research holds the potential to bring about the establishment of new frontiers. Researchers are on the verge of finally solving the mysteries that have eluded comprehension for centuries thanks to developments in technology, collaborations between scientists from different fields, and evolving paradigms in the scientific community. A paradigm shift toward a more systematic and evidence-based approach to paranormal investigation has occurred as a result of the integration of technologies that are at the cutting edge of technology, big data analytics, and ethical considerations.

It is the future of paranormal inquiry that invites us to transcend traditional boundaries, embrace skepticism and curiosity in equal measure, and embark on a journey that may redefine our understanding of reality. This is because the veil that separates the known from the unknown is beginning to thin. The pursuit of knowledge in the realm of the paranormal is a dynamic and evolving endeavor that bridges the gap between the mysterious and the empirical. This can be accomplished through, among other things, the exploration of haunted locations using advanced sensors, the analysis of patterns in large amounts of data, or the collaboration of researchers from different fields.

7.1 Emerging Fields: Integrating parapsychology and mainstream science

In the quest to understand the mysteries of the human mind and the unexplained phenomena that have fascinated humanity for centuries, the intersection of parapsychology and mainstream science represents a compelling frontier that represents a compelling frontier. Telepathy, precognition, and psychokinesis are just some of the unusual experiences that are investigated in the field of parapsychology, which is frequently regarded as a subfield of the scientific inquiry. The purpose of this investigation is to investigate the emerging fields that are bridging the gap between mainstream science and parapsychology. It also highlights the potential for a more integrated and nuanced understanding of the extraordinary aspects of human consciousness.

A historical perspective on the field of parapsychology

The foundations of parapsychology It was in the late 19th and early 20th centuries that the formal discipline of parapsychology came into existence. This was driven by a fascination with psychic phenomena and the desire to apply scientific methodologies to the study of the paranormal. Joseph B. Rhine and other pioneers laid the groundwork for the field of parapsychological research by conducting experiments that were considered to be landmarks in the field of extrasensory perception (ESP) and psychokinesis (PK).

The field of parapsychology encompasses a wide range of phenomena, such as telepathy, which is the communication of thoughts from one person to another, clairvoyance, which is the perception of information that is far away or hidden, precognition, which is the knowledge of future events, and psychokinesis, which is the movement of objects or events through the use of the mind. The purpose of these fields of research is to investigate the boundaries of human consciousness and to question the concepts of time, space, and causality that are commonly held.

Two of the Obstacles That Parapsychology Must Overcome

In spite of the fact that it has historical roots, the field of parapsychology has been subjected to persistent skepticism and stigma within the scientific community. A reluctance on the part of mainstream scientists to embrace parapsychological investigations can be attributed to the nature of paranormal phenomena, which frequently defies conventional explanations. There has been a marginalization of the field, with critics calling into question the dependability and replicability of the results of investigations.

There are a number of methodological challenges that are encountered in the field of parapsychological research. These challenges include the difficulty of standardizing experiments, the possibility of experimenter effects, and the elusive nature of the phenomenon that is being investigated.

The integration of parapsychology into mainstream scientific discourse has been hampered as a result of these challenges, which have contributed to the growth of skepticism.

A Shift in Perspective: Towards Integration

In recent years, there has been a gradual shift toward acknowledging the merits of parapsychology within mainstream scientific circles. This shift has been accompanied by a growing recognition of the field. An increasing number of researchers and institutions are coming to the realization that it is essential to investigate unusual occurrences using an empirical and open-minded methodology. Collaborations and investigations that span multiple disciplines have been made possible as a result of this shift.

As a result of its investigation of phenomena at the subatomic level, quantum physics has provided a theoretical framework that resonates with certain aspects of parapsychological phenomena. This is an example of the influence that quantum physics has had. There is a possibility that concepts such as non-locality and entanglement can provide insights into the interconnectedness that is observed in psychic experiences. These concepts challenge traditional notions of causality. There has been a growing appreciation for unconventional paradigms, which is reflected in the influence that quantum physics has had on parapsychology.

Interdisciplinary Collaboration: Overcoming Disadvantages and Disparities

In light of the fact that both mainstream psychology and parapsychology are concerned with gaining an understanding of the complexities of human consciousness, the integration of the two fields is a natural progression. Collaborations between psychologists and parapsychologists have the potential to contribute to a more nuanced exploration of the psychological factors that influence paranormal experiences, as well as the potential overlap between the abilities of psychics and cognitive processes.

Neuroscience and Abnormal Experiences: Recent developments in the field of neuroscience have made it possible to investigate the neural correlates of individuals who have experienced anomalous experiences. When researchers combine parapsychological investigations with neuroscientific methodologies, such as functional magnetic resonance imaging (fMRI) and electroencephalography (EEG), they have the potential to discover the neural mechanisms that are associated with telepathy, precognition, or altered states of consciousness.

In the field of quantum parapsychology, which is frequently referred to as quantum parapsychology, physicists and parapsychologists work together to investigate the possible connections that exist between quantum phenomena and psychic experiences.

While the purpose of these collaborations is to investigate whether quantum principles could provide a framework for understanding the non-local aspects of telepathy or the influence of consciousness on quantum systems, it is important to note that these investigations are speculative.

Regarding the Scientific Methods Employed in Parapsychology

Protocols for Experiments Parapsychologists are working to improve the rigor and replicability of their studies by refining experimental protocols. This is being done in an effort to address methodological concerns. It is becoming increasingly common practice in the field of parapsychological research to employ double-blind procedures, rigorous statistical analyses, and transparent reporting practices. These methodological enhancements contribute to the enhancement of the credibility of the findings of the experiment.

Meta-Analyses and Systematic Reviews: When it comes to evaluating the accumulated evidence from a body of parapsychological research, meta-analyses and systematic reviews are important tools to have at your disposal. Researchers are able to recognize patterns, evaluate the overall effect sizes, and provide a comprehensive perspective on the strength of the evidence for paranormal phenomena when they synthesize data from multiple studies and combine it into a single set.

The Relationship Between Parapsychology and Technological Advancements

Enhanced Capabilities of Parapsychological Investigations The incorporation of advanced sensor technologies, such as highly sensitive electromagnetic field (EMF) meters and biofeedback devices, enhances the capabilities of parapsychological investigations. Researchers are able to obtain more accurate measurements and real-time monitoring with the help of these tools, which in turn provides them with insights into the environmental factors that are associated with psychic phenomena.

Techniques of Neuroimaging: Recent developments in neuroimaging techniques, such as functional magnetic resonance imaging (MRI) and magnetoencephalography (MEG), have made it possible for researchers to investigate the neural correlates of people's experiences of psi. By analyzing the activity of the brain while performing telepathic or precognitive tasks, neuroscientists and parapsychologists may be able to discover patterns that are indicative of psychic abilities and improve our understanding of the relationship between the brain and the mind.

Ethical Considerations in Research Concerning Parapsychology Concerning

Well-Being of Participants: Ethical considerations in parapsychological research highlight the significance of participant well-being as an important factor.

In particular, given the possibility of individuals participating in experiments having experiences that are unusual or intense, researchers have a responsibility to place a high priority on the psychological and emotional well-being of those individuals. It is possible to contribute to ethical inquiry through the use of informed consent, debriefing procedures, and ongoing support mechanisms.

Transparency and Openness: In order to conduct ethical parapsychological research, it is necessary to report methodologies, results, and potential limitations in a transparent and open manner. Researchers have the ability to cultivate trust and credibility not only within the scientific community but also within the general public by adhering to rigorous research practices and maintaining clear communication with the public.

Public Opinion and Instruction

Participation of the Public: The incorporation of parapsychology and conventional scientific practices requires active participation from the general public. By demystifying the field of parapsychology, educating the public about the scientific methods that are used in parapsychological research, and encouraging critical thinking, we can contribute to a public perception that is more informed and supportive.

Science Communication: In order to bridge the gap between parapsychology and mainstream science, it is essential to maintain effective communication in the scientific community. Researchers have a responsibility to communicate their findings in a language that is easily understood, putting an emphasis on the empirical nature of their work while also acknowledging the various challenges that come with investigating paranormal phenomena. The facilitation of a dialogue that is more inclusive between scientists, skeptics, and the general public is facilitated by clear communication.

Prospective Paths and Opportunities for the Future

Further Integration with Mainstream Science The continuation of parapsychology's integration with mainstream science is the key to the field's growth and development in the future. A more comprehensive understanding of the human mind and the possibility of having experiences that are not typical will be achieved through the combined efforts of researchers from a variety of fields participating in collaborative research projects. The acceptance of parapsychological investigations will lead to an increase in the prevalence of interdisciplinary collaboration.

An Investigation into Consciousness Studies The combination of parapsychology and consciousness studies provides a rich environment for further investigation in the field of consciousness studies.

In order to shed light on the nature of human awareness, the boundaries of perception, and the possibilities that are inherent in expanded states of consciousness, it may be helpful to gain an understanding of the interaction between consciousness and paranormal phenomena.

International Perspectives and Cultural Sensitivity: In the future, research in the field of parapsychology should adopt a global perspective, taking into account the cultural diversity of experiences that are considered to be paranormal. Collaborations with researchers who come from a variety of cultural backgrounds will enrich the field by providing insights into the various ways in which psi phenomena are interpreted and manifested in different societies.

Continual Development of Advanced Technologies and Instrumentation The ongoing development of advanced technologies and instrumentation has the potential to refine and expand the methods that are used in parapsychological research. There will be an increase in the precision and reliability of studies as a result of innovations in sensor technologies, data analysis techniques, and experimental design. This will bring a new level of sophistication to the field.

As a transformative step toward unraveling the mysteries of human consciousness and the unexplained, the integration of parapsychology with mainstream science marks a significant milestone. As researchers attempt to navigate this frontier, they are met with obstacles, skepticism, and the requirement to adhere to rigorous methodological standards. In spite of this, the incorporation of parapsychology into the larger scientific discourse is being driven by the possibility of making ground-breaking discoveries and gaining a more profound comprehension of the extraordinary aspects of the mind.

Not only will the future of parapsychological research involve investigating the limits of the paranormal, but it will also involve expanding the boundaries of scientific inquiry itself. Researchers have the goal of navigating the intricate tapestry of human consciousness and the mysterious phenomena that lie beyond the grasp of conventional understanding. They plan to accomplish this by embracing collaboration, refining methodologies, and fostering ethical practices. As the integration of parapsychology and mainstream science continues to advance, it invites us to embark on a journey together in the direction of unraveling the mysteries that have captivated the human imagination for many generations.

7.2 Ethical Considerations: Balancing exploration with respect for the unknown

When it comes to the realm of paranormal investigation and exploration, ethical considerations play a crucial part in determining the course that research, investigations, and public engagement will take. In the process of navigating the mysterious terrain of the unknown, researchers are required to strike a balance between the pursuit of understanding and a profound respect for the individuals involved, the cultural contexts in which investigations take place, and the potential impact on larger communities. The purpose of this investigation is to delve into the ethical considerations that underpin research on the paranormal. It highlights the significance of preserving a delicate equilibrium between the pursuit of knowledge and the respectful acknowledgment of the mysteries that defy easy explanation.

Participant Health and Consent After Being Fully Informed

Prioritizing Mental and Emotional Health: The well-being of participants, particularly those who share their experiences with the paranormal, is an extremely important ethical consideration. When conducting research, it is imperative that researchers acknowledge the potential psychological and emotional impact of investigating phenomena that may challenge the beliefs of individuals or elicit intense feelings. It is imperative that measures be taken to prioritize mental health and that adequate support be provided both during and after investigations.

A fundamental component of conducting ethical research on the paranormal is obtaining the participant's informed consent. It is imperative that participants receive comprehensive information regarding the nature of the study, the potential risks and benefits, and the utilization of any data that is gathered. It is because of this transparency that individuals are able to voluntarily contribute to the research, comprehend the implications of their participation, and give their permission for the use of their experiences in scientific investigation.

On the other hand, openness and transparency in reporting

Open and Clear Communication with Participants It is of the utmost importance to keep an open and clear line of communication with the participants. Scientists are obligated to provide an explanation of their research methodologies, as well as the objectives of the study and the constraints of the research process. An open and honest line of communication fosters trust among participants and gives them the ability to make well-informed choices regarding their participation in paranormal investigations.

Investigating the paranormal in an ethical manner extends to the dissemination of findings, which is why transparent reporting in publications is essential. In order to uphold the principles of scientific integrity, researchers are required to report their methodologies, results, and any difficulties that they encountered while conducting the study in an open and honest manner.

It is possible for the scientific community and the general public to evaluate the credibility and reliability of the findings if a comprehensive account of the research process is provided.

Sensitivity to different cultures and inclusiveness

Beliefs and practices of different cultures are frequently encountered during the course of paranormal investigations. It is important to show respect for these beliefs and practices. Researchers have a responsibility to approach these cultural contexts with respect and sensitivity because ethical considerations require otherwise. For the purpose of avoiding unintentional disrespect or cultural insensitivity, it is essential to have a solid understanding of the significance of particular locations or practices within the context of local traditions.

Inclusion in Research Design: In order to conduct ethical research on the paranormal, it is important to make an effort to include everyone in the research design. That includes actively involving people from a variety of cultural backgrounds in the process of conducting research, beginning with the planning and execution stages and continuing all the way through to the interpretation of the findings. The use of an approach that is both diverse and inclusive promotes a more comprehensive understanding of paranormal experiences and lessens the likelihood of bias in the findings of research.

The Effects on Local Local Communities

Reducing the Potential for Harm to Communities: Investigations into the paranormal have the potential to have an effect on the communities in which they are conducted. Those conducting research have a responsibility to take into account the potential for harm, both psychological and societal, that their work may pose. Participation from the community, open communication, and the formulation of guidelines for respectful interaction with local residents are all potential strategies that could be utilized to reduce the potential for harm.

Finding a Balance Between Public Interest and Privacy The public's fascination with the paranormal frequently drives interest in investigations; however, researchers need to find a delicate balance between satisfying curiosity and respecting the privacy of individuals. It is important to have ethical guidelines that put an emphasis on privacy because the disclosure of personal information or locations without the consent of the individuals involved can result in unintended consequences for those involved.

Responsibility in the Representation of the Media

Avoiding Sensationalism: Ethical research on the paranormal extends to the representation of the subject in the media. In order to avoid sensationalism and the distortion of findings for the purpose of entertainment, researchers should be vigilant in terms of their approach.

Communication with the media that is conducted in a responsible manner ensures that the complexities of paranormal investigations are accurately portrayed, thereby reducing the risk of sensationalized narratives that may divert the attention of the general public.

Educational Outreach and Responsible Storytelling: Researchers have a moral obligation to engage in educational outreach that demystifies paranormal investigations. This kind of outreach would be considered responsible storytelling. The presentation of the scientific method, the inherent uncertainties in paranormal research, and the necessity of critical thinking are all components of responsible storytelling. In order to contribute to a more informed public discourse, researchers contribute by providing context and fostering scientific literacy.

A willingness to be skeptical and to consider alternative explanations

Extending a Warm Welcome to Critical Inquiry Skepticism is a fundamental component of the scientific method, and ethical paranormal research acknowledges its importance. It is important for researchers to actively encourage critical inquiry, constructive skepticism, and alternative explanations for phenomena that have been reported. The credibility of paranormal investigations is enhanced by the presence of transparency in the methodology used and a willingness to address any challenges that may arise.

Keeping a Healthy Balance Between Curiosity and Responsible Exploration Ethical considerations highlight the significance of maintaining a healthy balance between your curiosity and responsible exploration. It is essential for researchers to keep an open mind while simultaneously maintaining a commitment to rigorous scientific standards. At the same time, this equilibrium guarantees that investigations are carried out with honesty, which helps to cultivate an atmosphere of ethical inquiry within the sector.

Community Cooperation and Self-Determination

Collaborative Research with Communities: In order to conduct ethical research on the paranormal, it is necessary to work together with the communities that are being studied, rather than treating them as passive subjects. Individuals are given the ability to share their experiences on their own terms when they are given the opportunity to participate in dialogue, which involves seeking the input of community members and involving them in the research process.

Participants and Witnesses Should Be Empowered Throughout the Research Process It is important to empower witnesses and participants in paranormal investigations throughout the entire research process. It is the responsibility of researchers to maintain an atmosphere in which individuals are made to feel heard, respected, and valued.

Because of this empowerment, the study of the unknown is approached in a manner that is more ethical and accepting of all perspectives.

When it comes to the investigation of the supernatural, researchers are guided by ethical considerations as they navigate the complex dimensions of the unknown to find answers. It is essential, in order to keep the integrity of paranormal investigations intact, to strike a balance between the pursuit of knowledge and respect for the individuals involved, cultural sensitivities, and the potential impact on communities. Ethical principles serve as a compass for researchers as they delve deeper into mysteries that defy simple explanations. These principles ensure that the search for understanding is carried out in a manner that is transparent, responsible, and a profound acknowledgment of the mysteries that continue to captivate the human spirit.

7.3 The Uncharted Frontier: Inviting readers to continue their ethereal explorations

In the vast landscape of literature, there is a frontier that has not yet been explored, where the limits of imagination extend beyond the realms that are already known. It is a place where words transform into vessels, taking readers to ethereal realms that are not explored by traditional narratives. An invitation to embark on a journey of boundless possibilities and limitless horizons is extended to readers by this uncharted frontier, which is a call to the spirit of adventure that resides within each of us.

The promise of discovery is at the center of this vast literary expanse. It is a promise that reverberates through the corridors of creativity, encouraging readers to venture beyond the familiar and into the territories of the mind that have not yet been explored. If you are someone who craves the thrill of the unknown, the excitement of uncharted territories where the conventional rules of storytelling are bent, if not completely shattered, then this is a call to arms for you.

One of the most important aspects of this unexplored territory is its capacity to go beyond the mundane and to test the assumptions that people have about what constitutes meaningful storytelling. The realm in question is one in which the fantastical and the everyday coexist, resulting in the creation of stories that cannot be classified in any way. In this place, different genres blend together without any noticeable breaks, and the traditional boundaries of reality become a tangled web of otherworldly experiences and surreal landscapes.

There are a lot of similarities that can be drawn between this uncharted frontier and the great explorations that have been attempted in the past. There is a call for readers to explore the uncharted frontiers of literature, just as there is a call for daring explorers to set sail in order to discover new lands and map territories that have not been explored before.

The parallels go beyond the realm of mere metaphor, as both explorers and readers share a common desire to discover the unknown, a thirst for discovery that is not limited by the constraints of time or space.

This literary journey is centered on the idea of ethereal exploration, which can be described as a journey into the intangible realms of the mind, where ideas are formed and emotions are brought to life. In the course of these explorations, the uncharted frontier serves as a vessel, and it encourages readers to let go of the anchors of reality and set sail into the vast sea of imagination. Within the confines of this ethereal realm, the boundaries that separate the author and the reader disintegrate, and a mutually beneficial relationship develops, thereby establishing a shared space for the collaborative creation of worlds.

The fact that this uncharted frontier is able to accommodate a wide variety of voices and points of view is what makes it so inviting. Rather than being constrained by the constraints of a single narrative, it thrives on the variety of thought and the multiplicity of voices that are present in the world. In this vast body of literature, each and every reader assumes the role of an explorer, navigating their way through the unexplored regions of their own imaginations. The invitation is extended to everyone, regardless of their age, background, or experience; it is a democratic space in which the only requirement is a willingness to dream.

Instead of being a departure from reality, the uncharted frontier is more accurately described as an extension of reality. It is a manifestation of the human capacity to dream, to imagine worlds that are beyond the confines of the everyday. In the process of embarking on their ethereal explorations, readers are not evading reality but rather engaging with it in a different dimension. The frontier that has not yet been explored serves as a mirror that reflects the complexities of the human experience when viewed through the lens of imagination.

When it comes to this uncharted territory of literature, authors take on the role of cartographers, charting the contours of the imagination and leaving breadcrumbs for readers to follow. Due to the collaborative nature of this exploration, any two journeys will be completely different from one another. This is because every reader will bring their own distinct point of view to the unfolding narrative. The pages that make up the uncharted frontier are not static; rather, they are dynamic and responsive, transforming and adapting to the interpretations of those who travel through its landscapes.

As the reader progresses further into the uncharted frontier, they will find that they are confronted with the sublime and the surreal. It is a place where the laws of physics give way to the laws of storytelling, where the mundane is transformed into the magical, and where the ordinary is elevated to the extraordinary.

It is an invitation to witness the alchemy of words, where language transcends its utilitarian function and becomes a conduit for the extraordinary. The invitation to explore is an invitation to witness this magical process.

Nonetheless, the uncharted frontier is not devoid of difficulties to be overcome. In order to successfully navigate the twists and turns of narratives that defy conventional logic, it is necessary to develop a willingness to embrace the unknown. The reader is required to let go of their hold on the familiar and give in to the unpredictability of the imagination's currents in order to fully appreciate this. To put it another way, the uncharted frontier is not for those who are easily discouraged; rather, it is for those who are eager to experience the excitement of literary adventure and who are not afraid to confront the mysterious and the unexplained.

The uncharted frontier has the power to reawaken the dormant sense of wonder that resides within each of us, which is the source of its allure. It serves as a timely reminder that, regardless of how well-traveled the paths of literature may be, there are always new horizons waiting to be discovered. It is a celebration of the limitless creativity that characterizes the human spirit, and it is an affirmation of the infinite possibilities that are contained within the written word.

The uncharted frontier extends an open invitation to readers, encouraging them to continue their explorations of the ethereal realm. An invitation to embrace the unknown, to travel through the uncharted territories of the mind, and to take pleasure in the limitless possibilities that the imagination has to offer is being issued here. Not only do readers become passive recipients of narratives, but they also become active contributors to the construction of worlds as they embark on this journey through literature. The power of literature to inspire, to challenge, and to transport us to places we were unaware existed is demonstrated by the uncharted frontier, which is a testament to the enduring power of literature. Therefore, let the journey begin, and may the ethereal explorations of the uncharted frontier captivate and illuminate the minds of all those who have the courage to venture into its unexplored realms.